MEETINGS WITH AMAZING PEOPLE

WILL PARFITT

Will Parfitt has explored personal and spiritual development for more than forty years. Trained in Psychosynthesis and a Kabbalah teacher, Will lives in Glastonbury, England. He can be contacted via his website:

www.willparfitt.com

other books currently available
by the same author

FICTION
The Great Circle of Time
This Beautiful Garden

KABBALAH
The Complete Guide to the Kabbalah
Kabbalah: The Tree of Life
The New Kabbalah For Life

PSYCHOLOGY
The Something and Nothing of Death
Psychosynthesis: The Elements and Beyond
Psychosynthesis: New Perspectives (editor)
Walking Through Walls [Kindle]
The Elements of Psychosynthesis [Kindle]
Psychosynthesis: Beyond the Elements [Kindle]

MEETINGS WITH AMAZING PEOPLE

WILL PARFITT

PS AVALON
Glastonbury, England

© Will Parfitt

First published in the U.K. in 2017 by PS Avalon

PS Avalon
BM Synthesis
London, WC1N 3XX, U.K.
www.willparfitt.com

Will Parfitt asserts the moral right
to be identified as the author of this work

Design: Will Parfitt

*Front Cover Illustration: St Govan's Chapel in South West Wales,
a hermit's cell held sacred by Dorothy*

All rights reserved. No part of this publication may be reproduced, sorted in a retrieval system, or transmitted in any form or by any means, electronic, mechanical, photocopying, recording or otherwise, without the prior permission of the publisher, except in the case of brief quotations embodied in articles and reviews.

ISBN 978-0-9572246-8-1

Contents

Introduction 6

1 Anandapuran, a Messenger 8

2 Buddhism with Justin 27

3 Earth Magic with Seamus 41

4 Subud with Gabriel 57

5 Christianity with Ashe 69

6 Shamanism with Tomas 78

7 Kabbalah with Dafydd 100

8 Mysticism with Dorothy 115

Introduction

As a young man, when I came across the writing of the spiritual teacher Georges Gurdjieff I was very impressed. He wrote an autobiographical account of his youth and early explorations of consciousness entitled *Meetings with Remarkable Men*. Written as an adventure story but continuously bringing in spiritual truths from Gurdjieff's unique perspective on life, it describes various remarkable people who aided him in his search for hidden knowledge and spiritual wisdom. Blurring the lines between straightforward reporting, allegory and fantasy, he describes his encounters with monks, magicians, bohemians and yogis, and uncovers the truth he seeks. He describes a life lived to the full and centered on heart and purpose.

Gurdjieff's book had a deep impact on me when I read it in my early 20s and now, years later, I feel able to do my own version, describing some of the amazing people I met in the early days of my search for wisdom and understanding and who subtly – and sometimes not so subtly – set me on the spiritual path I have followed through life. I cannot know how much Gurdjieff changed his actual adventures to dramatize them but I have certainly done so. I have quoted Ursula Le Guin in one of my previous books (*The Great Circle of Time*) as saying: 'Experience is where the ideas come from. But a story isn't a mirror of what happened ... Truth includes but is not coextensive with fact. Truth in art is not imitation, but reincarnation.' This certainly applies to this book. I hope you can enjoy it in the spirit in which it has been created.

Note

Whilst the events described herein are true as I remember them and have recreated them, all the characters in this book, apart from the amazing people themselves, are figments of my imagination and not representations or characterisations of actual people. Some are based on real people, some are composites of various people, and some are pure invention. If you think anyone in here is you then you are mistaken. To put it another way, I'm not always sure I'm me, so you might just not be you!

1. Anandapuran, a Messenger

In the summer of 1974 I was living in Nottingham with my girlfriend, Marie. We had been together for a little over three years and our relationship was usually happy, or happy enough anyway. Marie was twenty-two, a couple of years younger than me, and striking in appearance, both by being tall for a woman – she was almost six foot – but also for having raven black hair that reached down to her waist. People who didn't know her well often assumed that Marie was very cool, but this outer coolness masked an intense sensitivity and, sometimes, deep anxiety.

The previous summer I had dropped out of an M.Ed. course and since then had been trying to make a living as a freelance writer. Mostly, though, I was still living a hippie lifestyle, spending long hours with friends, listening to music and putting the world to rights.

As I was expecting a visit from Rob, one of my hippie mates, when I opened the front door I was surprised by the short, thin Indian man in a slightly scruffy suit who stood before me. He carried a light brown, peculiarly small suitcase in his right hand.

"I've come to see you," he said, with a slight, almost smirking smile, "or more accurately I've been sent to see you." As he spoke I particularly noticed his dark blue eyes. I remember at the time thinking it sounded like a cliché, but I'd never seen eyes so large and bright before.

"Who sent you?" I asked.

"Ask me in and I'll show you."

I felt that didn't seem like the proper response, but being the good hippie I was at the time, I agreed to his request and invited him into my home. My hippie philosophy forbade me turning a stranger from the door, especially one with appealing blue eyes.

Marie looked rather nonplussed, to say the least, when I strode into the living room not with Rob but the Indian man. He immediately took the initiative.

"Ah, Marie, you must be Marie. I am so pleased to meet you," he said with a polite bow, clasping his hands together over his heart.

"And you are?" asked Marie.

"Sri Anandapuran." He said it very slowly as if spelling out each syllable. An-and-a-pu-ran. He didn't need to spell it out, though, for it is a name I will never forget, ever, not after what happened subsequent to this meeting.

Turning to me, Anandapuran spoke firmly and authoritatively. His voice was quite different from how it had been at the door. "I am here to tell your fortune, Will," he said, "but first we have to test the psychic energy between us. Are you willing?"

"Will it hurt?" I asked, half-jokingly. Apart from the possibility of a slight smile, Anandapuran didn't respond.

"What do I have to do?" I was starting to feel somewhat suspicious, paranoid about his motives.

"Nothing except sit down and answer a few questions. Please sit here next to Marie."

Marie was already sitting on the mattress on the floor, the usual hippie alternative to a sofa. She looked so cool I could tell she was very anxious, also from the way she was perched as if ready to jump up at the slightest provocation. I sat next to her, noticing both of us were agitated, sitting on the edge of our seats, breathing faster than normal. The atmosphere in the room felt charged, but with what I didn't know.

"Please relax," said Anandapuran, sitting cross legged on the floor a metre or so before the mattress. After rummaging in his suit pockets he took out a pencil and small notepad. Very seriously, half turning his back to me and making a big show of not letting me see, he wrote something on a sheet of his notepad, tore it out and screwed it up into a small, tight ball. I certainly had no idea what he had written.

"Here," said Anandapuran, "hold this tightly in the palm of your left hand. That's it, make a tight fist around it. You mustn't let me touch that paper again." He sat back and shuffled himself further away as if to emphasise his point.

I was feeling somewhat stupid for going along with this, that the whole thing was silly. "What's the point of all this?" I asked.

"Wait a moment. Think of a number."

"What?"

"Think of a number – a single digit number please."

This was now so obviously a trick of some kind but I didn't see any problem in going along with his game. I thought of the number 2.

"Have you got a number?"

"Yes."

"Do not tell me what it is, please. Now think of a fruit."

"Ah, c'mon!" I complained.

"Do as he said, Will," interrupted Marie who was clearly fascinated by what was happening.

"Okay." I felt determined to be difficult and came up with mango. As soon as I thought this, I mean immediately, or so it seemed, something was inside my head arguing with me, telling me to say apple instead. Feeling annoyed, I stubbornly changed my choice to orange. Now the voice inside my head became louder, only it wasn't a voice at all, more a compelling intent that I could not refuse. Choose apple it said resolutely.

Okay I thought, what difference does it make anyway. "Apple," I said.

Anandapuran showed no emotion at that moment. "Look at your piece of paper." His voice was cool and flat, but insistent too. He must have known of course, he wrote what was on the paper, but he wasn't going to lessen any impact through his foreknowledge.

Well of course I knew too – it just had to be. I was shaking all over as I unscrumpled the piece of paper that had not left my clenched left fist.

"What does it say?" Anandapuran was smiling now.

"Two. Apple."

Marie and I looked at one another and I think our jaws literally dropped. I immediately started wondering how Anandapuran did the trick, and how he had seemed to be inside my mind.

"Do not worry about how it happened, simply marvel at s the fact such events can happen. We are not really here to consider and discuss the mystery of life but to live it. What is a trick anyway?" Anandapuran paused for a moment. "Isn't all this a trick?" he asked as he swept his arms in a wide arc to indicate, well, everything. "The point is, we are now psychically attuned and I can disclose certain events from your future for you."

Anandapuran rummaged through the pockets of his suit jacket again, pulling out more pieces of paper than you'd think such pockets could hold. These papers were all rather scruffy and some of them Anandapuran cast to one side whilst making a distasteful tutting sound. Other pieces he unfolded and smoothed out with his hands, then lay on the floor between me and him. On these sheets were charts of various kinds, mostly consisting of squares in columns with what I assumed were Sanskrit letters in the columns. One of the laid out crumpled pages looked like an astrological chart, but like old ones I'd seen in books with, rather than a circle, a square with diamond and triangle shapes representing the signs and houses.

"That's an astrological chart, isn't it?" I asked.

"Oh yes, for this moment now. Our meeting."

"But how could that be? You couldn't have known beforehand that we'd be here at this moment."

"I didn't know, but I trust in the unfoldment of things."

"What do you mean?"

"Well, I was brought here by all this –" so saying, his hand swept over the papers strewn on the floor around him. "My choice, their choice, what's the difference?"

"Who are they?" I asked.

He did not answer my question, but, after making a sort of huffing noise, said, "Let's get on with your fortune, please."

I still felt sceptical. It seemed an over-elaborate routine for a door to door salesman, which after all was what Anandapuran looked like in his scruffy suit and with his little suitcase. The number and fruit thing was a clever trick, and he clearly had an intriguing and powerful presence, but I was still on guard. Marie seemed to be lapping it all up and I felt rather jealous of the rapt attention she was giving Anandapuran.

"Enough of this," Anandapuran said commandingly, engaging my vision with his strong blue eyes. He seemed to penetrate into me. It didn't feel like I was being hypnotised, I'd have resisted that, but there was nothing to resist, nothing to do but enjoy the cool warmth of his gaze. I know that doesn't make sense, but that's how it felt, like a cool warmth.

"Firstly," said Anandapuran, "you will be moving, but in the opposite direction than expected."

"You mean not to Wales then?" asked Marie excitedly.

Anandapuran glanced momentarily at her and said somewhat dismissively, "I just bring the messages, I do not interpret them." His strong eyes re-engaged my vision. It was as if he had never been gone. At that moment it felt as if we had always been together, feeling joy together that was not like an orgasm but more like the best moment of the relaxed feeling after one.

"Second, you will remain financially sound so long as you circulate and act with truth." Before I could ask him to clarify that, he continued. "No, I don't know what that means exactly, but that's the message. Circulate and act with truth. There is that which comes and that which goes.

"Thirdly, you will find a vital link through someone whose been closer to you than anyone else ever could be.

"Finally, one more prediction which you mustn't share with anyone ever." So I'm not going to, but the prediction continues to come true.

Anandapuran started gathering up his papers and stuffing them back into his pockets.

"Is that it?" I asked. I was not very impressed by his predictions – I was going to move in a different direction than expected, my money situation would be okay so long as I circulate and act with truth, or words to that effect, and someone close to me would give me a vital link, whatever that meant. It was all pretty general sounding and the final prediction (the one I cannot reveal) was just too weird and abstract.

What about meeting a tall dark stranger, I thought somewhat cynically. But at the same time, I was also feeling the impact of the words and activities of the short dark stranger sitting before me on my living room floor.

Having gathered up all his papers, Anandapuran stood up and, picking up his suitcase, placed it on a chair and opened it. "There is one other thing," he said deliberately. He took out of his suitcase a square of yellow Indian cloth about a meter across, made of good heavy quality material, embroidered with a pattern using gold thread, and with golden tassels around the four sides. It looked quite splendid, and rather expensive.

Was this the dénouement, I thought, was this what his show had been about, to sell us a piece of cloth?

Not at all. Handing me the cloth, Anandapuran said carefully, "This is one of a pair. This one is for you. The other one is in safe keeping and you will see it later." He continued by making a big fuss of how much of a pleasure it had been to meet us, then made to leave. Somewhat reeling from all this, and still clutching the yellow cloth, I followed him to the front door.

"Will we meet again?" I asked.

"We all meet from time to time," he replied with a smile, and held out his hand.

As I took his hand in a handshake, I felt a strong electric current pass from him to me. Just for a moment it seemed as though I saw the world through his eyes. I don't mean I was in him, I was still completely me, but as if I literally had his eyes in my eye sockets. The world was sparkling and everything was tinged in a deep blue. Then he was gone.

I went back into the living room. "What do you make of that?" I asked Marie as I sat down next to her on the mattress and passed over the yellow cloth.

"I really don't know," she replied, holding the material up and admiring it greatly. "And you know, he didn't try to sell us anything. I mean, it was all so strange. I'm not sure I'd even believe it happened, except look, I'm holding this beautiful, Indian, embroidered cloth."

"The piece that is mine, " I said, taking the cloth back and holding it up to the light. "What was that he said, about another piece that is in safe keeping, or something like that. Weird!"

*

Rob, the friend I had been expecting when Anandapuran visited, never turned up. But the next day, I had another unexpected visitor, a mutual acquaintance of Rob's and mine called Lucy. In fact, Marie and I only vaguely knew Lucy as the girlfriend of Seth, an older hippie. I had heard he was in prison and I was not surprised, I'd never been comfortable in his presence. But Lucy, a blonde woman of about my age who was pretty but not beautiful, seemed okay on the whole and not caught up with various illegal activities like her boyfriend. She had a slight lisp and a strange habit of frequently opening her eyes extra wide and sort of staring but not looking at you directly. It was disconcerting but somewhat appealing too. It was the first time she had ever visited Marie and me on her own and I was curious as to why.

"Thing is," she said, sitting on the mattress settee, "I don't want to stay in Nottingham any more, not now Seth's inside, and I want to make a new life. Anyway, I found this really nice cottage in the Yorkshire moors. Rob told me you guys were wanting to move and there's this other empty cottage next door to mine and I wondered if you'd be interested."

Marie and I looked at one another with amazement. "In the north east," Marie said incredulously.

Lucy of course, didn't understand why we were acting this way. "Look, well it is the north east, but it's Yorkshire and it is lovely up there, they are not all Geordies or anything, and some people say it is much better than Wales, for example." She burbled on some more till I stopped her.

"No, listen Lucy, it sounds great. We'd have to look first of course. We were just thinking we were moving to the south west and –" I paused and gave Marie a knowing look, " – and just yesterday someone said to us perhaps we'd move in the opposite direction than we're expecting, then you turn up today and suggest the north east rather than the south west."

Lucy looked perplexed.

"The north east is the opposite direction from the south west in a compass," Marie said helpfully.

"No, I get that," said Lucy. "Funny thing is, I was originally thinking about the south west too, until I heard about this place. So, are you going to come up and look?"

Of course we did, and about two months later we moved to a lovely cottage on the edge of the Yorkshire moors. Situated outside the village of Button, the cottage was luxurious for Marie and I who had lived in a one bedroom flat in Nottingham. We not only had three bedrooms (one of which we made into a temple), dining room, living room, bathroom, kitchen, outhouse, coal shed and greenhouse, but also about half an acre of garden with a small fruit orchard beyond. Best of all, however, we just couldn't believe our luck, the rent was half what we had been paying for the flat in Nottingham. Lucy's cottage and ours were originally tied farm workers' cottages, not needed for such labour since the mechanisation of agriculture. It was actually in our agreement that if the buildings were ever needed for workers, we would have to vacate. I still remember the farmer, our landlord Mr. Burns, tapping contentedly on the bonnet of his Mercedes and assuring us this would never happen.

So we had somehow been led to this relatively idyllic life in the north east of England. Was this anything at all to do with Anandapuran's prediction? In one sense, Marie and I wanted desperately to believe it was, but in reality we were convinced it was a coincidence, that we had discovered the place through Lucy. How could it really be otherwise? Living next door to Lucy turned out, at least in the early days, to be pretty good. She was good fun and even when we noticed she occasionally stole odd things from our kitchen (like a couple of potatoes, or a box of brillo!) we didn't really mind.

*

At that time, I was an avid reader of books on all different aspects of the esoteric and occult, so soon after moving I joined the local library in the nearest small town, which was called Ayley. In those days, you could order books from the whole library system of the country and, sometimes after a short wait, they would be delivered to your local library for you to borrow. I used to scour the bibliographies in books I enjoyed, and then order many of the titles that appealed to me. As I remember, they were quite generous in the Yorkshire library service and I was allowed to order perhaps as many as ten titles at any one time. I made full use of this wonderful free service.

One of the very first books that arrived for me to collect from my local library in Ayley was *The Serpent Power* by Sir John Woodroofe (also known as Arthur Avalon.) It was a rather learned but also instructive book about tantra, a method of using energy, particularly sexual energy, through different breathing techniques and the like, to attain altered states, or at least that was how I viewed it then. I'd been wanting to read this book for quite a while so as I left the library felt very happy to have a copy of it in my hands at last.

The library placed a simple cardboard bookmark in all the books that were borrowed through the interlibrary service. It had something on it about looking after the book carefully, and there was a space for the librarian to write in the date of its expected return. Nothing else was usually ever written on these bookmarks. Today was different, though, I remember it vividly now. I was exiting the library door and, eagerly opening the book at the page where the bookmark was inserted, I almost dropped the book in total surprise when I saw, written in clear handwriting across the bottom of the bookmark 'Anandapuran.'

Rushing back into the library, no doubt with a crazed air about me, I keenly wagged the bookmark before the young woman assistant who had served me. "Did you write this on here?" I asked excitedly.

She looked at the bookmark with bemusement. No. I wrote the date," she said, "but the anand – whatever, no. Wait a minute." She turned and called to the other woman who worked in the library and asked if she had written it, which, of course, she had not. "I don't know how it got here, sorry, " the librarian said, returning to me. "Do you want a new bookmark without scribble on it?"

"Oh no." I quickly took the bookmark back. "No thanks, I want this one very much."

They must have thought I was crazy, then and many times afterwards. I never really could tell what these young librarians felt about my reading pursuits, from The Serpent Power through all kinds of books on magic and the occult.

Marie was naturally also intrigued by the mystery. How had Anandapuran's name come to be written on the bookmark? How could it be anything else but proof that his prediction about our move to the North East was meaningful, and not just a lucky guess or coincidence? Yet how on earth his name had been literally written on the bookmark remained a mystery. Interestingly, though, through the Serpent Power book itself, I did learn something of Anandapuran's name: 'puran' means unity or oneness, and 'ananda' means bliss. We found out Anandapuran is the bliss of oneness (or the oneness of bliss.)

*

The next proof of Anandapuran's predictive ability turned out to be even more astonishing. A year or so after living next door to Lucy, she came rushing round to our house one morning with exciting news. "Seth is coming out in two weeks!" she exclaimed noisily. "Two weeks! I've so much to prepare, but isn't it wonderful. Wonderful!" It wasn't just her words, her whole body spoke in exclamation points.

I took Lucy's hands and, steering her out onto the front lawn, I started jumping up and down with her. "Wonderful it is wonderful," I cried. Lucy became ecstatic, jumping up and down with me and exclaiming even more.

Truth is, although I might have been happy for Lucy, I felt very ambivalent about Seth's homecoming. The few times we had previously met, I'd never really liked his attitude, far too cocky. He was very tall, well over six foot and with a slim build. Most striking though was his long, curly ginger hair with which he incessantly played, stroking or pulling at strands of hair in an admiring sort of way. Apart from any of that, though, my worst fear concerned Seth's behaviour – he wasn't in prison for nothing. I wasn't altogether sure but I knew it was at least his second time inside, and he'd probably done more. I never knew exactly what were his crimes, but as they involved prison I assumed they were serious. What he might be going to introduce into our now tranquil country life, I dreaded to think.

I tried my best to stay positive. Marie was convinced that if we kept a positive attitude everything would turn out fine, but I wasn't so sure. On the day he came home, however, I was genuinely pleased to see Seth, albeit only briefly before he and Lucy retreated into their own, obviously much needed, couple's space.

Marie and I were invited round the following afternoon for tea. When we went in, it was obvious that Lucy and Seth had been too engrossed in themselves to think about anything else. They were so happy, it was a joy to be there with them. We all sat round the glowing log fire, enjoying the good feelings associated with Seth's safe and happy homecoming. At that moment his past didn't matter to me at all, nor to him I imagine.

"You collect some interesting bits and bobs inside," said Seth, reaching for a medium sized cardboard box near his seat. "I haven't shown you these yet, honeypie," he said to Lucy, "my prison booty! Look at this first." Reaching into the box and somewhat furtively taking an object out, he passed her a small, green soapstone Buddha which she gleefully took and held to her as if he had given her the most precious gift, which of course in fact he had.

"This is the best, though," Seth said, reaching into his box and pulling out the identical piece of yellow Indian cloth given to me by Anandapuran. Marie and I both audibly gasped.

"Yes, it's beautiful isn't it," said Seth, believing we were gasping at the cloth's beauty rather than just the fact of its appearance. I was literally speechless for a moment or two; I stopped thinking or feeling anything, it was as if just me and that piece of cloth existed in the universe, or not even that, just the yellow cloth of which I was only a part, or, even more true, the weave and web of which we are all part.

Next thing I knew I was lying on the floor with Marie, Lucy and Seth attending to me. I had fainted for the first and only time in my life, to that time anyway. Well of course we told Lucy and Seth about our piece of cloth. Marie went next door to fetch it, and they did indeed perfectly match. Seth couldn't exactly say when he had acquired his piece, he had swapped another prisoner some tobacco to get it, he said. This was surprising, he added, because his tobacco was very precious to him in prison, but he had fallen in love with and just had to have this cloth. From what he said it was not impossible he had received it on the very same day I'd received mine.

"The other one is in safe keeping," said Marie.

We all looked at her quizzically.

"That's what he meant, Will," she explained. "Don't you remember what Anandapuran said when he gave you the material. 'This one is for you, the other one is in safe keeping.'"

I still didn't fully twig. "So Seth has been keeping it safe?" I asked, bemused.

"No, listen. In safe keeping, it was in safe keeping. Prison. The material was in prison. How could he have known that?" But then, how could he have known any of this?

*

For the first couple of years living in Yorkshire, life for Marie and I was wonderful. Our only concern was money. Marie had a job at a local health shop which brought us a small regular income, whilst I worked as a freelance writer and my earnings were at best sporadic and sometimes near non-existent. I frequently ruminated on Anandapuran's words that I would always have enough money if I continued 'to circulate and act with truth.' I had no idea what this really meant, and as I often didn't feel as if I had enough money anyway, Anandapuran's statement was meaningless to me.

Around the same time that Seth came back from prison, Marie and I were in a particularly poor financial state, brought to a head by Marie being made redundant from the shop where she worked. I had suggested to Marie on a couple of similar occasions that perhaps we should first spend all the money we had and trust that something would turn up, but in the end we always backed off what was, rationally, a silly thing to do. It was Marie who raised the subject this time, though. We had just less than one hundred pounds in total to our name (which had greater value in those days, but still wasn't really very much.) Marie said she was determined to buy a new pair of boots out of this money, whatever it cost. I also badly needed some new jeans so we felt we could justify a shopping trip and that we would take all our money and spend everything we needed to spend without concern for what would or wouldn't be left.

We were both excited by the prospect and the day we set off for York, which was the nearest city with lots of shops, we were jumping for joy. Perhaps we faced financial ruin, but we were going to have one last day of total abandon. We agreed to separate to do our own shopping, then meet at a café in the centre of town at one o'clock. That gave us almost two hours shopping before lunch, which was more than I thought I would need anyway. I think Marie was concerned it wouldn't be enough.

I was pleased it didn't take me long to buy my jeans, so I had plenty of time to scour second-hand record shops, one of my favourite hobbies at the time. I hadn't paid much attention to my jeans costing £9.99 but I was amused when I paid £1.11 for a record then £5.55 for several records in another shop. When I bought some chocolate, tobacco, rolling papers and matches in a newsagent's shop and the bill came to £2.22 I was really amazed and mystified.

At about five past one I arrived at the café where Marie and I had arranged to meet. I was already somewhat fazed by the synchronous prices of my purchases that morning but imagine my total surprise on finding Anandapuran sitting at a table with Marie!

"What on earth…?" I said as I arrived at the table. "I mean, how…"

Marie shrugged her shoulders in a 'don't ask me' sort of way, and appeared to be in the same state of shock as me.

"Sit down, Will," said Anandapuran, rising from his chair and pulling an adjacent chair out from under the table for me to sit on. Speaking almost too formally he said, "I'm so pleased to meet you again."

"I'm pleased to meet you, too," I responded, "but what are you doing here? How did you know Marie and I would be in York today?"

"Let me assure you that I did not know you would be here anymore that you knew I would be here. The spirit has brought us together at just the right moment, that's all." He smiled. "Simple if you know how."

"What?"

"You moved, you saw the second yellow cloth, now today you are here bringing money to circulate and act with truth. It isn't something you can comprehend with the normal way of looking at things, but I assure you until I saw Marie outside this café a few minutes ago, I had no idea I would see you today."

"We did seem to just bump into each other outside, Will," said Marie as if to corroborate his story.

I thought for a few moments. This was a lot to take in. "But how did you know we'd moved, and I'd seen the cloth, and about our decision to spend money here today?"

"I just know that as we've met again you must have fulfilled the prophecies from our previous meeting. That's how it always seems to work. I have something else to tell you now."

I don't know how long she had been there, but at that moment I noticed the waitress standing besides the table with a bemused look on her face. Marie and I ordered a drink, Anandapuran said he didn't want anything just then.

After the waitress left, Anandapuran continued. "There are seven people to date that you have interacted with who have each brought you a piece of exquisite wisdom. Right now, you may remember some of them or not, but your task is to recall your meetings with each of these amazing people in detail, and what you were taught. Someone general will help you to remember the final person who you will find you never forgot."

"Someone general? What does that mean?" I asked.

"I do not know, but that's the message – you'll meet someone general."

"Who are you, Sri Anandapuran?"

A friend, a friend of yours, and of everyone of us. I'm a messenger, that's all really."

So saying, Anandapuran stood up as if to leave. I stood too. "You can't go, you have to explain more, tell me who you are and what this remembering people is about. What's this all about?" I felt really agitated.

"It's not about anything, Will," said Anandapuran calmly, "it just is what is. Remembering the people will tell you what you need to know."

"But what if I don't remember the right people? I've met lots of amazing people in my life."

"That's not really an issue, you will remember the right ones. If you were not going to, then why bother to send me with the message?"

"Who sent you?"

"No one sends anyone anywhere, Will. It just is what is."

I just knew there was nothing else to say. Marie and I bade Anandapuran farewell and he left us in the café. We sat quietly for quite a while, sipping our drinks silently and reflecting.

I then remembered the co-incidence of the price of my purchases and having the three figures repeated for each. £9.99. £5.55. £2.22. I excitedly told Marie of this.

"Look at this!" she exclaimed, reaching into her hand bag and pulling out a sales chit – yes, a new pair of boots for £55.50.

To cap it all, the following morning in the post I received a letter commissioning me, with a substantial fee, to write a product manual for a large company, and Marie received a letter offering her a new and better paid job than she had applied for.

In the coming period, Marie and I often reflected on what Anandapuran had taught us. Firstly, by the prediction that we were going to move in the opposite direction than expected, we learned to expect the unexpected. We immediately saw how that was a lot more exciting way to live.

Secondly, through seeing the second yellow cloth we learned that things can be connected even when apparently not so, that there is a web of connection that doesn't depend upon our usual perceptions of time and space.

Thirdly, through circulating money with an act of truth we could ensure we had enough money. 'What you give out you get back' applies to money and, conversely, if you try to hold onto it, you end up losing it. The act of truth was to trust in 'the universe' to provide so long as we stay in the flow of things. Why, money is even circular in shape, as if to remind us of this.

Finally, and best of all, the act of truth, our trust and abandon to the flow of life, led us to our meeting in York with Anandapuran.

I set about my task of remembering the seven people with a lot of glee, some trepidation and not a little anxiety. What could all this mean? What was going to happen when I remembered everyone, assuming I could? And who – or what – was this 'someone general' who would help me remember the most important person of all?

2. Buddhism with Justin

Justin, who I met when I was seventeen, was clearly one of the seven people I was charged with remembering. It was 1967 and I was still living at home in Cardiff with my parents, and felt moody most of the time. I did not have a girlfriend and was dying to explore my sexuality, but as if that wasn't enough, I had hit some kind of spiritual crisis following a powerful individuation process a few months earlier. This experience had been so luminous, the whole world lit up and I felt as if a heavy cloud had been lifted from me. Everything following it seemed dull and meaningless by comparison. Studying at school, religion, the chatter of friends, all simply made life feel empty and without purpose or meaning.

This sudden illumination followed two years of quite intense and very painful teenage depression. I had literally felt like a dark cloud hung over me whilst everyone else was out in the sunshine. Although I'd rejected religion, my desperation drove me to prayer. Every night before sleep, and in the morning upon waking, I followed a simple prayer regime. Making myself as peaceful as possible, I praised God, said I was sorry for all I had done wrong, thanked God for all the good things in my life, and then I asked for the cloud to be lifted away. My attempt at covering all the angles was in the hope that something would get through to whomever or whatever He was, if He existed at all.

I can't recall what exactly happened, but what I remember is that one morning, an hour or two after rising, I noticed that the sun was shining above my head. The black cloud was no longer there. My heart filled with joy and, for the first time in my life, I felt a deep sense of freedom. The experience lasted for a day or so. The light didn't leave, but the everyday world intruded back into my awareness, and how mundane everything seemed. Although the process had lifted my depression, it did not leave me with any sense of connectedness. I had awoken, for sure, but to an almost unbearable loneliness. Perhaps because I was a teenager, the only solution that came to mind was to have a girlfriend, to become sexually involved, but I was too shy. The cloud may have lifted from my inner self, as it were, but on the outer I lacked confidence that I was okay, especially to the young women I most fancied.

In an attempt to meet someone, I started attending various meetings such as a local scientific society, a youth club, and a couple of poetry and folk clubs. It was at a poetry club that I first met Justin. The club was in the upstairs room of a pub, had its own little bar and that evening I drank rather too much. I think the two friends I had gone with were in a similar state. I don't know how we started talking, but I found myself sharing quite intimately with a man a few years older than me. Justin was rather handsome with his dark curly hair and Mexican-style moustache. It was the summer of love in San Francisco, but in Cardiff at that time, Justin's bohemian dress was not yet out of fashion, and he looked really cool. He wore a brightly coloured, open-necked shirt and had tied a scarf around his neck in a rather flamboyant manner. His tight black trousers and black boots with elastic gussets completed the picture. What I liked was that although we'd only just met, I felt that Justin was really listening to me. In my drunken state I blurted out my sorrows, my lack of a love life, and my sense of meaninglessness about everything. I really appreciated his attentiveness, his knowing nods, his understanding responses. When Justin asked if I wanted a lift home in his car, I was only too glad to accept.

Justin was lovely a man and I felt there was no problem in accepting his lift, not that I think I would have cared, or even noticed, that night if there had been. He only lived a few streets away from my parent's house and knew the way to my street. Very few words passed between us as he drove across town. He parked outside my home and, saying thank you, I went to leave his car.

"What you need is Buddhism," he said softly. I wasn't quite sure I'd heard him properly so, turning back towards him, I asked him to repeat himself. "What you need is Buddhism," he said once more.

Of course I knew a little of Buddhism from religious studies at school, but I had no idea what Justin could possibly mean. I'm not sure I even realised one had a choice of religions. I asked him to explain what he meant.

"You are full of desire, Will. Life is full of suffering and it is all caused by desire. Stop desiring and you stop suffering."
"But how can we stop desiring things? It's impossible. I mean, for example, didn't you desire this car when you bought it?"
"Of course I wanted it. Actually you are right, I really desired it. But that's because I'm not there yet. I still suffer, oh you bet I do. But the thing is, you can work on stopping the desire to stop the suffering."
"How?"
"Through what Buddha called right conduct. All that means, basically, is living as honest, compassionate and harmless a life as possible. Also we can meditate, and then meditation can lead to desire disappearing, release from suffering, and eventually even enlightenment."

I was drunk, remember, but somehow his words made me feel even more drunk. I just couldn't take it, and saying I needed to urgently pee, excused myself and went indoors.

*

Whilst in the school library the next day, I remembered what Justin had said about me needing Buddhism, so I decided to at least give it some consideration and searched out a book on the subject. From that first book, whose title I do not remember, I learned that Buddhism had been around for about two and a half thousand years. It was not surprising to learn therefore that it had lots of different schools with different ideas and practices. Some Buddhists seemed to literally worship Buddha as God whereas others seemed to believe that we are all buddhas. Some thought enlightenment comes in a flash; others believe you have to work at it. What the book didn't really tell me, or at least I couldn't understand, was what Buddhism was really about, or why Justin said I needed it. I felt totally confused and yet my appetite was whetted.

The following week, at the end of the poetry club, I jumped at the opportunity of another lift from Justin. I quickly told him of my confusion and asked him to tell me what he had meant.

"There's three things all Buddhists believe in," said Justin. "The Buddha, the dharma and the sangha."

I thought I might have come across these words in my reading but I had no idea what they meant. Justin made it all sound easy.

"The dharma is the essence of Buddha's teachings," Justin explained. "We live a continuing cycle of death and rebirth and our well-being is determined by our behaviour in previous lives. So long as we remain attached to the cycle of death and rebirth, we can never be free from pain and suffering."

"That's heavy," I said.

"Yes, but that's what I was telling you before. There is a way out, or through, the world. All we have to do is stop desiring things, or at least stop being attached to worldly things. By ridding ourselves of attachment, we reach enlightenment."

I wasn't at all sure what the difference was between desiring something and being attached to it. Justin instantly picked up my uncertainty.

"It's simple, Will," he said, "all you have to do is follow the middle way, doing nothing extreme, just allowing the flow of life. That way you can avoid both uncontrolled desire and lust and, at the other end, self-denial and self-torture. Buddha intended us to be in the world, to find enlightenment through being honest, doing nothing to hurt others, respecting other people and their lives, their opinions, their property. Just being mindful of what you do and don't do in your life, which is of course pretty difficult but it starts becoming easier as you go along."

"That's a lot to take in," I said. "I don't think I could make it, I'd fail all the time. I'm always desiring things, I'm attached to a good life, I want sex, I want money, I want success, I want ..."

Justine interrupted my flow. "But you don't have to succeed, Will, that's not the point. It's engaging with the practice, it is the going not the goal that matters."

"But there is a goal," I countered. "Enlightenment, you just said so."

"Well, yes, sort of, but the goal can only be found through letting go of all desire, including the desire to reach the goal."

He flummoxed me there. I thought we'd better move on. "What's the other thing you said, sangha something?" I asked.

"Yes, sangha. It means the community, everyone who is following Buddhist beliefs, whether a full time monk or ordinary folk. The idea is that if you have a community of like-minded souls around you it offers both challenge and support. Anyway, sometimes it is nice to just have people around."

"But, Justin," I said with exasperation, "this is all talk, isn't it? What about all these different schools of Buddhism? What sort of community is that? And how on earth do you meditate, and what does it all mean?" Truth was, I liked all he was saying, it made sense to me on a deep inner level, but I just couldn't see how it was relevant to my life.

"Well, Will, you're right," he replied, "and I'm not saying another word. This is all words, indeed. You need experience, that's how you get to Buddhahood, not through talking about it."

"So what do you suggest?"

"I have some papers from my teacher that are very practical, I'd like to share his teachings with you. If you are at the club next week, we could meet again afterwards if you like. Perhaps we could go for a drink before I drive you home?"

"I thought Buddhists didn't take intoxicants!" I exclaimed.

"I told you I'm not perfect," he countered.

*

We didn't go to a pub because Justin had left the papers he'd promised me at his flat and suggested we go straight there instead. Justin's flat actually consisted of a small bed-sitting room with an even smaller kitchenette attached. The bathroom and toilet, out in the hall, were shared with other flats. Despite its size and limitations, though, Justin had created a paradise of colour and lighting effects that turned the main room into a rich, sumptuous den. He boyfully showed me the control box he had rigged up so that he could switch the eight different lights in the room on and off from his bedside. I never knew before that where the shadows overlap from different coloured lights, they blend together to create a new coloured effect. I was overwhelmed.

After putting on some cool jazz music, Justin left me playing with his light controller whilst he went into his kitchen to make some tea. I was happily sitting on his bed playing with the lights when I suddenly realised this could all be a set up, some gay seduction scene. I wasn't sure what I felt about that, but I liked Justin a lot and, quite honestly, at that moment felt open for anything. If this was all a ruse to get me here and seduce me, then so be it. I was both excited and nervous, but when Justin returned with the tea he was so normal and straightforward my fears were quickly forgotten, especially so when he took a wadge of papers out of a drawer and handed them to me.

"I've duplicated a copy of these special teachings for you, Will," said Justin. "I hope you will accept them as freely as they are given."

I was delighted. At that moment I felt I was being given the greatest gift possible, and perhaps I really was. I tried to thank Justin but he wouldn't have any of it.

"These aren't mine to give, these words belong to the universe. Thank the universe Will, that we have met so they have come your way."

I really didn't know what to say and started to look at the pages.

Justin quickly stopped me. "Put those copies in your bag, Will, so you remember to take them away. We can look at my originals. I'd like to go through some of the teaching with you, if that is okay with you?"

I readily agreed and Justin took out a folder that he had rather beautifully painted with little Buddha images, and put it on the bed.

"The best thing," said Justin, broadly smiling at me, "would be for us to now smoke charge."

"Smoke charge," I repeated quizzically. I had no idea what he meant.

"Yes, you know, charge, shit, weed. Cannabis."

I had tried smoking cannabis at a couple of parties and my mother's hairdresser had once turned me on when I was about fifteen, but I wasn't particularly keen. In these circumstances with this wonderful man who knew so much about my new passion, for so Buddhism was becoming, I would agree to anything. It was unnecessary, but Justin even explained to me how cannabis isn't an intoxicant that is proscribed by the Buddhist precepts, which translated properly says not to take any intoxicant that removes the sense of awareness and attention.

"So, said Justin triumphantly, "it is fine to use charge because it increases your sense of awareness and attention."

I wasn't fully convinced by his argument but I didn't give a damn. "Go ahead, " I said, noting this cool new word I'd learned for cannabis – charge.

I don't know if it was the company or the strength of the drug, or most likely a combination of both, but it certainly did increase my awareness and attention. I sat wide eyed watching Justin almost turn into a Buddha himself as he rapped for what seemed like hours about this special teaching, a story as told him, he said, by his teacher. I heard each word he spoke clearly formed as if spoken by a master linguist. Yet Justin actually spoke in quite a small, quiet voice. As for the meaning, I struggle to understand a little of the mysteries now many years later, but that evening every word of Justin's speech carried a tremendous significance and had an overall enlightening effect.

I didn't realize it at the time but I think now that both Justin and I were in a trance.

Maybe it was because I was stoned, the power of Justin's

story, a combination of the two or what, I'm still not sure, but I vividly remember much of what he told me that night.

"There are just a few things you need to know and if you know these, you know everything you will ever need to know. First things first, Will, that's the way. First you have to learn to face life as it is, learning always by direct and personal experience. If someone shoots you then you wouldn't ask who the man was or how the bullet was made before concerning yourself with getting the bullet out of your body.

"Secondly," said Justin dramatically as he spread his arms wide and gestured to indicate the surroundings, his cleverly lit room with its opulent feel. "These things, too, will pass away. Everything changes, everything that exists from a bit of dirt in the gutter to a mountain, from an ant to a human and beyond, nothing lasts for ever. If it is born it may grow and if it grows it will decay and what decays then dies. That's true of everything, life is a flow and if you resist the flow you suffer. Cling to absolutely nothing.

"There may or may not be an ultimate reality which is immortal and unchanging, but there is no soul or principle in an individual which doesn't change and cease. We don't own our life energy anymore than we own the air we breathe, anymore than a light bulb owns the electricity that lights it up."

Justin often paused between these assertions to toke on the joint and sip water. I just sat there transfixed by all the wisdom he was sharing.

"Everything we experience, all our circumstances we create for ourselves, how we respond to current circumstances has a causal effect on our future in this life and our future destiny in successive lives. Only through right thought and right action can we purify ourselves and attain freedom from rebirth. It takes a very long time and we have to be patient though. In fact if we wait long enough everything living and non-living will reach ultimate enlightenment.

"Next, realize that although there are innumerable life forms which all must die, life itself is one and indivisible. We are all on the same bus travelling through the same universe, and when you think that way it is natural then to be compassionate, to want to live in harmony with your fellow travellers. If you break the harmony of life you delay your enlightenment. Selfishness produces suffering, whereas sharing and compassion reduce suffering. Desire produces suffering and the elimination of desire removes suffering. Only the ignorant strive for their own desires at the expense of others.

"The path to enlightenment is a way of living not a theory of life. Learn to do good things and be clean in your heart."

I remember at that point Justin stopped as we both contemplated what being clean in your heart might really mean.

"Reality is indescribable but Buddha taught us that when you look inside you find you are Buddha, so keep becoming more what you are rather than what you are not.

"We have to develop our thinking, feeling and sensing, our heart and mind must both be developed, so as we develop we become more whole. The best way to do this is to tread the middle way, doing nothing to extremes.

"If we practice mindfulness, looking inwards, meditating, having regular periods of quiet, we become more balanced in our lives. We can refrain from becoming attached and see life as the show it is. We become aware of how we are ourselves, and how everything we experience is our own creation so there is no need for us to overreact to any experience, whatever it is – and if we do react, to not beat ourselves up over it.

"Finally, no prayers will work unless you walk your talk, unless you are true to your fellow man and most importantly to yourself. We are each ultimately our own authority. We have no right to interfere with a fellow traveller's journey. Don't be dogmatic, be tolerant, even if you do not understand your friends' or enemies' beliefs. We each have the fullest right to put our own meaning on life. When we look inside we find we can be self-reliant, practical and all embracing of otherness."

I was stunned by the simplicity and the truth of all this. Justin was still smiling broadly as he leant forward and, attempting to kiss me, put his hand onto my genitals. What an immediate and shocking come-down this was for me. Justin could have easily seduced me that night if he hadn't come on so quickly, but at that moment I was spiritualized not sexualized. His description of the Buddhist path had had a powerful effect, as if bringing me to myself. He had just described exactly what I felt I'd been struggling to find for myself. Justin was apologizing but I would have none of it. Picking up my bag, I left speedily and dramatically.

*

I occasionally saw Justin around after that but we never spoke. I didn't know what to say to him and I think he felt too embarrassed or ashamed to speak to me. A little while later I heard he had gone to India on a spiritual quest and I hope he found what he was looking for. The best thing Justin had taught me was how insignificant we each are and how compassion can open the heart and help us come together. It did not matter to me at all about his seduction attempt. It wasn't that I forgave him for there was nothing for me to forgive. Rather I thanked Justin for showing me so much, and sent blessings to him on his path. If I judged him then, because we are all in the same boat really, then I also judged myself.

On top of this, there was the great gift of the papers he had so deliberately put in my bag when I was at his flat. I don't know whether he consciously knew what he was doing, I guess not, but it meant that whatever happened that evening I left with the papers, because most certainly when I left after the seduction attempt, I wouldn't have remembered to pick them up. It's a strange dharma transmission, as a Buddhist might call it, but for me it really was the transmission of an ancient teaching.

These written teachings were supposedly from his teacher, but I don't know if they were or whether he wrote them himself because some years later I discovered they were a re-worded extract from the Tibetan Book of the Great Liberation. I also discovered sometime later that the principles he had also ascribed to his teacher were actually based on the Twelve Principles of Buddhism composed by Christmas Humphries, a distinguished judge and founder of the London Buddhist Society. Whatever, all of Justin's teachings had a great and positive effect on my life. I lived with the words from the Book of the Great Liberation for several years, even as my interest went elsewhere, and throughout my life there have been many occasions when I have been drawn back to these words to re-read them, particularly the following extracts:

Only in the present moment you can understand an empty Mind. Empty the Mind now and all that remains is the present moment, here and now. When you seek the Mind in its true state, although invisible it is completely intelligible. In this true state Mind is naked and clean: void, vacuous and transparent; without duality;

timeless, unimpaired, unimpeded, colourless. It is not realizable as a separate thing but as a unity of all things, yet not composed of them. Your own Mind is not separable from other minds. Every number is infinite; there is no difference.

There being nothing to meditate upon, there is no meditation needed. Similarly, there being nothing to go astray, there is no going astray. Without meditating, without going astray, look into the true state of the Mind, where self-recognition, self-knowledge and self-illumination shine endlessly. Realize your self radiant, self born wisdom.

All concepts are illusions, none of them real, they all fade away. All things perceived are concepts. Ignorance and misery are concepts. Self originating divine wisdom is a concept. Good or bad fortune are concepts. One pointedness is a concept. Qualities are forms are concepts. Existence and non existence as well as the non-created, all are concepts of the Mind. Liberation from concepts is a choice which is also a concept.

Nothing but Mind is conceivable. There is nothing conceivable that is not Mind. Mind, when free, conceives all that comes into existence. That which comes into existence is like the wave of an ocean.

No matter what name you give it, apart from Mind there is nothing else. This unique one Mind is without root or foundation.

There is nothing else to be realised.

*

Nirvana, according to Buddhist belief, is a state of perfect peace and blessedness. The attainment of nirvana enables us to escape from the painful and continuous cycles of death and rebirth which only end when all our desires are completely eliminated. Buddha taught that nirvana can be attained by following a Middle Way between self-indulgence and self-denial, and by practicing the Noble Eightfold Path which consists of correct living, including proper behaviour, proper meditation, and proper insight into truth. Whatever Justin's behaviour, his inspiration taught me to at least aspire to these principles, but he also taught me that that even when we do not measure up to these principles we do not fail.

Zen Buddhism teaches that enlightenment can be attained through direct intuitive insight. Some followers of Zen believe that this enlightenment must be achieved gradually through a long process of self-discipline, meditation, and instruction whilst others believe it comes in a sudden flash of insight. To the seventeen-year-old I was at that time, the latter opinion was certainly the more attractive, especially when compared with practices that seemed to take years. The pop Zen of the 1960s gave the impression that desire could be stopped in an instant rather than through continuous hard work. My inner Buddhist self (or perhaps no-self!) paradoxically led me away from Buddhism and towards other paths to instant enlightenment.

3. Earth Magic with Seamus

I met Seamus through Tom the Tune, one of the most outlandish hippies I knew during the late Sixties. Tom was certainly an amazing guy himself, but in a much more negative way. He lacked the good heart energy that I discovered in all of the seven people who brought me 'a piece of exquisite wisdom', as Anandapuran had described they would. Even Justin, despite the seduction attempt, was a heartful person who always intended the best (even if it did not always work out that way.) Tom was not so endowed and in fact, behind the peace and love façade was one of the most calculating and duplicitous people I have ever met. One time when I was away visiting my parents, he told some crooks he knew who consequently burgled my flat. Tom of course received a share of the proceeds. How I found that out some time later is another story altogether. Of course I challenged Tom about it but he didn't show any remorse or offer an apology – he was more concerned with dissing the other person who had told me he was involved. He also asserted the hippie ideology about property being theft, so I was a bad person for being concerned about it!

Tom and his girlfriend Mandy were living in an allotment shed at the time, but not at just any allotments. Hunger Hills in Nottingham was set over several rolling hills and much of the area had gone wild. Whilst some allotments, particularly near the edge, were well tended and what you might call typical with their tidy rows of vegetables defying the tireless encroachment of a wide variety of weeds, a deeper exploration into the overgrown heart of Hunger Hills revealed many surprises. Tom and Mandy's home was one such surprise: set amidst a copse of wildly overgrown fruit trees, Tom had added a wooded extension onto an old allotment hut and made a two room abode for him and Mandy. From the outside it looked little more than a repaired allotment shed, but, inside, the walls were covered with old carpets to keep it warm, whilst the floor of the latter half of the accommodation (which in total probably measured less than five meters square) was covered with two mattresses and layers of flash cushions. There was even a wood burning stove in one corner with hot water nearly always at the ready for tea. Whilst the holes Tom dug outside in various places to provide toilet facilities were as basic as you could get, it somehow suited the hippie 'back to nature' ethos by which they at least partially lived. Several other hippies, including some good friends of mine, also lived at the allotments, but none had such a well-developed home as Tom and Mandy.

At the time I was still a student (in name if not in application) and Tom loved to share with me his interesting finds at Hunger Hills allotments. More than anything, he did this for his own amusement, somehow sneering at me all the while and, when other people were involved, making fun of them in an unkind manner. He always managed to disguise his remarks in such a way that it was impossible to be sure if he really meant what he seemed to say or it was just me interpreting it that way. Of course if he was ever challenged, Tom stuck to his love and peace, common-wealth stance. I must say, though, some of Tom's discoveries were quite amazing. There was Josie, for instance, an older hippie woman who lived in a nearby allotment shed and who would resolutely not talk to Tom or any of his friends and cursed and swore at us if we ever approached her; Nick and June, a harmless pair of peace-and-love hippies who lived in a hut second only to Tom's for its opulence; an allotment with chickens and large hand-written signs warning of gun traps for the unwary thief – Tom, assuring me the guns were real, claimed to have stolen one and I believed him; and the always unlocked back door to a house on the nearby estate where the people were out all day and where Tom collected his water supplies (of course without them knowing.)

On the particular day that Tom took me to meet Seamus I was expecting nothing more than another hippie drop-out. Seamus, however, turned out to be considerably older, greying and maybe in his mid-forties, and rather incongruously he was always impeccably dressed in an old but clean dark blue suit with polished brown brogues on his feet. Short and stocky, slightly bent over yet wiry too, he matched for me the stereotype I had of what an Irish man should look like. Tom had described him as a crazy old Irishman, and at first that was exactly what I took him for. He lived, apparently, in one of the big houses that bordered one edge of Hunger Hills but, also according to Tom, he was always at his allotment whatever time of day – or night – you went to look. I wasn't sure that Tom was correct, though, because the first thing I noticed was that there appeared to be no work at all done on the allotment, it was one of the most overgrown looking of them all.

When Tom introduced us that day, Seamus was very polite with him but slightly standoffish. With me, he didn't seem to care one way or the other whether we had met or not and, surprisingly, I found that refreshing. I see now this was because his greeting was so different from the overly positive ones hippies frequently gave but which weren't really genuinely backed up with feelings as strong as the message of love and peace suggested. Tom made some off-hand remark about Seamus being a professor of botany and when I inquired what he meant, he said that Seamus knew absolutely everything about every plant. Although I had learned very little despite studying botany in the school and university system, I nevertheless felt very sceptical that this little

Irishman could know so much and expressed this.

Responding to my scepticism, Tom turned to Seamus. "Go on, Seamus," he said, "show Will what I mean."

Seamus just sideways smiled and said nothing.

"Do you know a lot about plants?" I asked.

"Oh, just a little, a very little," he replied.

"Go on then, Seamus, what's this tree here?" said Tom rather sharply.

I thought Seamus gave Tom such a terrible look and then suddenly his face changed and he replied. "You would call it elder."

Now I really am not very good at recognising trees, but I know – and I'm sure Seamus knew – that elders are really common trees and many people can easily identify them, especially when they are in bloom or when they are covered with berries. Of course, Tom didn't know that he had picked a very easy tree for Seamus to identify.

"I don't think I'd call it anything, Seamus," Tom replied sneeringly.

As it was May, the tree was particularly splendid, covered as it was with creamy-white fragrant blossoms. I wanted to know more and asked Seamus what else he knew about the elder tree.

For the first time, I think, he looked me straight in the eye. "Do you really want to know about the elder?"

His eyes were beautiful and soft and I'd have said yes even if I meant no, but by now I really did want to know, not so much about the elder tree but about this unusual Irish man.

Turning towards the tree and speaking softly in his small, measured voice, he announced: "The elder." He paused momentarily before continuing, as if saying a silent prayer.

"The elder heralds the beginning of summer when it is in blossom and the end of summer when it is covered with berries." Despite his very strong Irish accent he spoke so slowly and carefully that each word sounded clearly. All three of us moved closer to the tree and Seamus put his hand gently on the bark. "Look," he said, "look closely at the body of this tree. This is the most generous of trees to both human and the other folk."

I asked him what he meant by the other folk but he ignored my question. I don't remember all the things Seamus said about the elder tree on that first meeting, but his knowledge was truly astounding. What I do remember is how he carefully explained each part of the tree had a specific use. He claimed that if the properties of its leaves, flowers, bark and berries were fully known we could fetch a remedy for any ailment or sickness from the one tree. Apparently English people used to call it the medicine tree in older cultures, and Irish people always raise their hat when passing an elder tree in blossom or when it is carrying berries.

Seamus took some leaves from the tree, thanking its spirit as he did so, and then bruised the leaves quite roughly. Handing some to both Tom and I, he told us to rub our faces with the leaves and no flies would settle on us. "Of course it would be better to make an infusion of the leaves with a jug of hot water and leave them for a few hours. You can use such an infusion to keep away all flies, midges, mosquitoes and the like."

I was impressed and certainly didn't know this before. Tom seemed rather more sceptical and maintained his sneering attitude, but Seamus ignored him and continued. "Course we cannot pick the flowers now," he said, "because they must be in full bloom and they ain't quite there yet. You then can throw them into heaps, after a few hours they become slightly heated then you can remove the flowers more easily and sift through them for debris, insects and so on. Actually most of the insects will have left, they don't like it getting too hot in there." Seamus was warming to his subject and rubbed his hands together rather gleefully as he described the insects scuttling away.

"To use the flowers you have to make elderflower water, it smells bad to start but the more you cook you know its ready when it starts to smell sweet. It's used for making medicines, for the eyes and skin, it's good if you're sunburnt. You wash your hands with it and your lady's face. In fact if you like a woman with a nice white body then just sneak some of it in her bath."
We all laughed, men together, knowingly.

"Elderflower tea is a good laxative too," Seamus continued, and a good cure for the flu. You have to keep drinking it once you know you have it, then it's gone sooner, that's all."

It's great for piles too, I can tell you!" he suddenly exclaimed. I don't think I'd ever heard anyone express anything about piles before and really warmed to this character.

"Tell us about your piles, Seamus," Tom said, but Seamus didn't fall for this.

"Well, there's the berries too, when they come in autumn, they're wonderful. You can make wine from them that's really healing, see you right through the year, and a thick rob that is warming on cold winter days. That'll stop any rheumatism, and if you have it hot before going to sleep it will help with sore throats and colds and the like, all good stuff for your chest.

"Then there's the bark, when you collect that in autumn you can make something from it that promotes longevity, it's so sweet at first, then bitter and nauseous. I've been sick on it many times, it really purges you. And the roots, even, they –"

Tom cut Seamus short. "Don't get too carried away now, Seamus, you'll be telling us all your secrets," he said, laughing.

"We have to go now, anyway."

"Those weren't secrets," said Seamus, perhaps for the first time slightly rattled by Tom's attitude. Then he turned to me: "But I could tell you a few," he said softly and slowly.

Tom ignored him. "Another time, old man," he said, "we gotta go now. C'mon Will."

*

When we returned to his abode, Tom gleefully regaled Mandy with impressions of Seamus instructing me on the use of the elder, and mimicked my interest by standing on one foot, and looking dumb, mouth wide open. Tom clearly did not perceive what I saw and seemed to have no real interest in Seamus. Sadly, I think this was because for Tom only people who had something he could either leech off or steal from were worth anything and Seamus clearly didn't have any money or possessions. For me, though, Seamus seemed to possess something I had been looking for, something worth more than any money, a genuine connection with nature and a deep wisdom beyond the words and concepts of my Christian upbringing or my then currently held pop-Buddhist beliefs. At the earliest opportunity I visited Hunger Hills again and looked out Seamus for myself.

Seamus's allotment was actually quite hard to find in the maze of overgrown lanes that made up Hunger Hills. I felt foolish, I didn't know why I was visiting him, nor even if he would be there. I remember arguing with myself and feeling irritated all the way there. I almost turned back several times. I'm so glad I didn't though, because my contact with Seamus was going to forever change my perceptions of the world – or I should say worlds – in which we live.

When I arrived, I could have sworn Seamus had a robin perched on his left hand and he seemed to be having a conversation with the bird which, upon my arrival, flew into a nearby tree. I was amazed by what I'd seen but Seamus dismissed my excitement, claiming I must have been seeing things. He said he had just been holding an old piece of bark which he had then thrown into nearby bushes. I couldn't be one hundred per cent sure, but his slow, convincing words seemed genuine and perhaps I had been seeing things.

Seamus wasn't going to leave it at that, though. "So you like seeing things, do you, Will?" he asked, slowly forming the words in a way that made them seem almost menacing.

"Yes. Depends what you mean, though," I replied cautiously.

Seamus appeared to change the subject. "Do you remember all the things I told you that we could use the Elder for?" he asked.

"Some of it," I answered honestly. In fact he had shared so many possibilities for the elder tree I remembered little of it, but I had retained some of his wisdom. I started blurting out to Seamus how I had been astounded, not only because his knowledge was so rich but also because it highlighted for me yet again how woefully inadequate my school education had been. I studied Botany for eight years in total, right to advanced and university level, but never had heard of these uses for the elder tree before.

Seamus response was down-to-earth. "You can even make a seat out of it," he said, laughing and pointing to a 'bench' beside his allotment hut. "Let's sit down."

I was happy to be asked to sit with Seamus. I immediately had a very strong positive projection onto him. He had an unusual energy about him, and with his short stature and bent, wiry appearance there was something pixie or elf-like about him. I don't remember thinking this at the time, but I honestly believe now he may have been half human, half leprechaun! What was most striking about Seamus, though, was his beautiful smile that was a permanent feature on his bony face. If I feel myself now going more than half way towards a full smiling face, I feel that's where Seamus's smile started.

Seamus told me that Hunger Hills was originally called Hanging Hills because Celtic pilgrims used to come there to a holy spring and hang pieces of cloth on nearby trees so the wind could spread their blessings. When I asked him if the spring was still there, he looked at me quite strangely at first then asked me if I would tell Tom where it was located if he told me. I thought of Tom stealing into someone's house each day to collect his water and suddenly realised the paradox in his supposed back to nature lifestyle. I could easily assure Seamus that I wouldn't reveal the spring's whereabouts to Tom or anyone. Seamus just listened but did not respond, and in fact only showed me the spring many months later.

That day we sat silently for a short while, both facing to one edge of his allotment where the ground sloped downwards quite sharply. I noticed a small area of tended ground with vegetables growing there which were well hidden until you noticed them. Beyond the copse of elder and hazel trees at the bottom of the allotment I could see the hazy rooftops of Nottingham. It was a beautiful, sunny day. I felt the rays of the sun warming my face and healing my soul and felt at one with nature. All I could hear were the sounds of many different birds busily singing in the morning warmth. More distantly a dog barked and some children were playing, maybe in a school playground on the nearest estate. A pigeon or two coo-ed nearby and I felt this was the peace I had yearned for all my life, what should have followed my earlier transcendent experiences. The silence seemed to last forever until Seamus finally broke it.

"We live in paradise and we are surrounded by abundance," he said carefully.

Just that, no more. I was transfixed. What had been transcendent, beautiful in a trippy sort of way, now had become sensitised, raw, and edgy. Over and above all the other sounds now, my hearing focussed solely on the sound of Seamus's breath. It was loud, distinct, regular, relaxed, and relaxing. Nothing had changed, I still had the same view ahead of me of the allotment, trees, and rooftops, but now I felt part of it and it part of me. Looking around me in the mostly overgrown allotment I perceived the most glorious treasures. Every plant, every part of every plant had its purpose, equal to and part of the same purpose of which I am part. There's really no way to fully describe the experience in words.

Seamus repeated the phrase, now softly spoken but commanding: "We live in paradise and we are surrounded by abundance."

A wave of paranoia hit me – was this a seduction scene? Was Seamus another Justin, was this all about sex?

It was as if Seamus read my mind because the knowledge that this wasn't a seduction came clearly into my mind, just as if Seamus had spoken. When I asked him about it later, he always maintained that he was not mind reading, he was using the faculty we all have to body-read each other. It didn't matter at that time, anyway, because the words had the desired effect. I felt calm again and, just at that moment, a large black mongrel dog came bounding into the allotment and diverted our attention.

"Toby," said Seamus leaping up and embracing the dog

who wagged his tail wildly and jumped up happily to meet Seamus's embrace.

"Who's this?" asked Toby, turning to me.

I nearly feel off my seat. What was happening to me? A talking dog!

"Who's this?" said Seamus, turning to face me. "This is my friend Toby. Toby, meet Will."

Toby slowly walked up to me and I tried to gently reach out to pat him but I was shaking too much to move.

Toby licked my hand and I felt myself relax again. I could hear his breathing, just the same way I had heard Seamus's before, regular and relaxed. For a moment nothing existed but the sound of Toby's breath, then I realised it was Seamus's breath I was listening to, that we were both still sitting on the elder bench besides his hut.

"And before you ask," said Seamus, turning to me and smiling very broadly, "dogs do not talk."

"What –"

Seamus cut me off with a sternly raised finger. "There's no need for talk just now. We can talk more next time you come to see me."

*

This was my first deep experience of the immanent spirit alive in everything. I had been performing Zen practices but had not really achieved this state. All the way home and all evening I tried to remember the phrase Seamus had used. The best I came up with was: 'I live in paradise and I am surrounded by abundance.' It didn't sound quite right, but was still a very magical saying so I started repeating it to myself over and over. Just being alive was being in paradise, I realised, and in my lucky, Western lifestyle of the late 1960s and '70s I was surrounded by abundance, an abundance of positive, inspiring energy that was perfect for me at my age. I had already taken lsd and cannabis, and yet as wonderful as these drugs were, they did not match the totally relaxed splendour of Seamus's allotment that afternoon. I couldn't wait to see Seamus again to ask him how he made this happen, I so longed to know. I determined to go see him again the very next day.

It was about 10.30 when I arrived. Being May the sun was already quite high but the bench at the side of Seamus's hut was completely in the shade. I was half expecting to see him sitting there and felt a little disappointed that he was not. In fact, as I looked around, it appeared no one was there. Seamus's hut was not locked, so after tapping the door I looked inside and discovered it was a proper, scruffy allotment hut with a few old tools in it, just as it should be. Nothing at all like Tom and Mandy's palatial hut.

Not sure what to do, but hoping that Seamus might show up soon, I moseyed about, picking at this and that. I sat for a while drinking from the water bottle I'd brought in my back pack. I tried meditating but couldn't quite settle enough. Finally, more out of boredom at waiting than anything else, I took a hoe from the hut and started hoeing between the rows of various vegetables Seamus had planted in the small cleared patch semi-hidden near one edge of his allotment. I was out in the open here, so I became very hot and soon stopped my work and walked back to the hut to get my backpack and water. It was gone. I started panicking, wondering what to do, when I heard Seamus's voice from round the side of the hut.

"It's round here," he said quite distinctly.

I felt so relieved that my pack had not been stolen.

Apart from the water, it had my wallet in it, plus various other possessions. Bounding round the side of the hut, I stopped dead in my tracks. Sitting on the bench next to my bag was not Seamus but Toby.

"Better in the shade," he said. I realised his voice sounded quite like a dog barking really, and started convincing myself that I was just imagining Toby was talking but he was really barking. He looked at me expectantly. Walking up to the bench, I took the water from my bag and drank long from its contents. I offered Toby some which he lapped from my cupped hand. He then jumped off the bench, invited me to sit down with a nod of his head, and ran out of view. I did as I was told and a few moments later Seamus appeared from the other direction than Toby had gone.

"How did you do that?" I asked excitedly.

"Do what?"

"You know what, Toby was here with my bag and he spoke and –"

Seamus cut me off. "Toby is part of my imagination, Will, that's all. We live in paradise and are surrounded by abundance. That's all."

I realised something that has stayed with me as a vital understanding all my life since, something that becomes deeper and deeper in meaning the more I contemplate it. For a moment I felt completely enlightened. When I had tried to remember his affirmation, in my version, I had used 'I' rather than 'we'.

"How do you do it, Seamus?" I asked again.

"It's simple, listen again: we live in paradise and we are surrounded by abundance."

I told Seamus how I had remembered it wrongly.

"That's the whole point, Will," he told me. "It is not that

you are bad or wrong or anything like that, you are like all humans in the modern world, you live by ego, the I, from the I to the I, round the I, it's all I. I of the I. Until you shift your consciousness to the 'we' you are trapped in your own limited bubble. Join the 'we' as we are all connected, all one." He stopped and looked at me long and hard then repeated the words once more in his slow clear Irish voice. "We live in paradise and we are surrounded by abundance."

"Is it as simple as saying those words then?" I asked.

"Not really. You have to achieve its consciousness. We can show you the way but you cannot take it until you are ready."

"What should I do first?"

"Seriously. Take off all your clothes and roll in the earth. From the earth we all come and we all return, are really all one. Do it now."

Realising that he really was deadly serious, I took off my clothes and lowered myself onto a piece of the ground that had been dug over but no yet planted. I felt frightened of the worms and bugs and beetles touching my body, but that fear was soon over-ridden by the joy of lying naked on the earth. I started to roll as instructed and was soon rolling merrily over and over, feeling at one with the earth in a previously unimaginable and blissful way.

I still roll on the earth to this day, whenever I get the chance. But strangely, until Anandapuran instructed me to remember these amazing people I had met, I'd never really realised the great gift Seamus had given me that day.

I carried on seeing him for the rest of the time I lived in Nottingham, not regularly, more often than not visiting his allotment whenever I felt I needed a boost of positive energy and a 'top up' as it were of his natural earth teachings. Seamus told me all he shared with me was from the Celtic tradition of his family and homeland and always asserted he was a poor representative of the teachings that, he claimed, all true Irish people understand. The essence was very clear even to a non-Irish person like myself: that all beings are interconnected through being part of the earth and it is through connecting to the earth that we can truly live in abundance. Of that, Seamus was the perfect example by being, on the surface, an average, even poor, Irishman who had nothing and yet, truly, was as rich in spirit as anyone could be and who, through his deep connection to nature, was a truly amazing person.

*

The last time I saw Seamus, after we settled on his bench with Toby by our side, he told me he was returning to his home in the South West of Ireland. His wife had died suddenly and he felt very alone. I was truly shocked as, although I'd known him for quite some time by then, I had no idea he was married. I had always seen him alone, apart from that first meeting through Tom, and he had never talked of his life outside of our meetings at his allotment. I expressed my concern and asked him if there was anything I could do.

"You can be my witness here, because I'm not going to share this with anyone else now. I was here when she died. She had been ill for a few days, coughing and the like, but it didn't seem more than a passing cold. Sitting on our bench here, I saw her fly across the sky from East to West and I knew."

"You knew she had died," I said.

"I knew I had to return to the West, that I knew." He paused, tears welling up in his eyes. "I also knew I would never return home so long as she was alive, so yes, I knew that too."

"What did you do?"

"I went to our house, called the doctor, a respiratory thing he said, her lungs had collapsed. Nothing could be done. I knew that."

We sat silently for a while. I didn't really know what to say and, although I didn't know it at the time, of course saying nothing was exactly the right thing.

Finally, I broke the silence. "You must miss her a lot," I said.

Seamus looked deeply into me. Toby was by his side, his nuzzle resting on his master's knee. "She's waiting for me in the West," Seamus said. "In the West," he repeated, looking now into the distance, westwards. "Nothing ever changes, really, only the surface of things, not the spirit. I cannot really miss someone who I've never really ever been parted from."

I believed at the time I knew what he meant. It was much later, only after remembering the seventh amazing person I was asked to recall, that I truly understood the depth of feeling, and meaning, in his words.

4. Subud with Gabriel

I had my first contact with the third person of the seven even before I had left Cardiff to go to university, but it was sometime later before our contact brought him into the realm of amazing people in my life. At the time of first meeting with Gabriel, I was taking my advanced level exams at school with the aim of securing a university place, but my interests had moved elsewhere. I was called for an interview by the university which had been my lowest choice on the application form. The interview must have gone well because at the end they offered me a place, but with one condition, that I take a year off first. I was gobsmacked, it was a dream come true.

I believe they thought that if I had a year off I would get my rebelliousness out and would be able to settle down better to university study. My parents responded really well to this and generously supported me in having the year off. The school wasn't too happy but there was nothing they could do about it, and as for my school mates, well, there were a lot of green faces. Now I could devote all my time to my pleasure pursuits! I had a great year, doing the occasional odd job, but mostly hanging out with friends, and particularly girlfriends. The house being empty during the daytime whilst my parents were at work, I found plenty of scope to explore this special interest.

One day I was roaming through some nearby streets in Cardiff with Phil, a dear friend at the time, and we saw that the front door of a typical Victorian semi had been brightly painted with blue and yellow stripes. We had never seen anything like it before and, being the proto-hippies that we were, we plucked up the courage to go tap on the door and see if anyone was in.

A very smartly dressed middle-aged man came to the door, not at all what we expected. In fact, he was one of the smartest men I had ever seen, his dark suit was obviously expensively tailored and he was immaculate in every way. He had silver grey hair and a smartly trimmed short goatee beard. Although a little shorter than me, he stood very upright and appeared tall, creating quite an imposing presence.

His eyes gleamed with life when we asked about his painted front door. "Oh my son painted that," he said, laughing. "I'm never sure what I think about it – do you like it?"

We said we did, had some short conversation about art that I do not remember, and fairly quickly left. This man made a big impression on me but at that time I had no idea how influential he was going to be. It happened through his son whom I met quite separately. His name was 'Sergeant' Pepper, or so everyone called him. Over the period of the rest of my gap year we became quite friendly and when I went off to university, agreed to maintain our friendship. Pepper told me that he was leaving his flat and going to stay at his father's for a while so gave me the address to visit him next time I returned to Cardiff.

It was the Christmas holiday of my first term and I was back home. Keen to see Pepper, I went to the address he had given me and, to my surprise, it was the house with the painted door. Of course, I had not known the address so had never had any reason to connect Pepper with this unusual house. It was Pepper who had painted the door. He was as amazed as me about the co-incidence when I told him about meeting his father, but, at a later date, he told me he had asked his dad about it and he couldn't remember the incident. This was not surprising really and I thought no more of Pepper's father until a few months later (in the Easter recess, I think) when he answered the door when I was calling for Pepper.

"Haven't I seen you before?" he asked.

I told him about the time I had called and he obviously remembered it now. "I remember Pepper asking me, well I remember now I see you. Welcome to our home." So saying, he held out his hand for a handshake (which seemed rather old fashioned at the time) and invited me in.

We went into the kitchen where I expected to see Pepper but Gabriel (for that was Pepper's father's name, I now knew) explained that his son had had to go away. "But you must stay for a cup of tea," said Gabriel amiably, pulling out a chair for me to sit at the dining table. I felt a little uncomfortable, I liked this man but he was my friend's father and I felt a generation gap difference. I respected him though and somewhat reluctantly sat down. I couldn't find anything to say to him and I felt the silence between us becoming acutely difficult.

We were sitting at the table supping the tea he had made, which was, incidentally, my introduction to mint tea which for years I had as my drink of choice. Finally, Gabriel spoke: "Do you know Subud?" he asked.

I had no idea what on earth he was referring to, and in fact had to ask him to say it a few times whilst I tried to understand what he was saying. It seemed rather weird, but finally I got that it was an acronym, Subud being short for Susila, Budhi and Dharma. Not that I was any wiser, but, wanting to appear more knowledgeable than I was, I suggested that he was referring to the three-fold way of Buddhism that I'd learned from Justin.

"The Buddha, his teachings and the community of Buddhists," I said.

"No, not exactly, not really, that's Buddhism and Subud is not about any religion or believing anything. It's quite simple: Susila means to be able to live according to divine will, to live as a real human being. Budhi means that within us is a Divine Power which works within us and without us. Dharma is the possibility of completely surrendering to the divine will. If you put these three together, Subud, it simply means to follow the will, the divine both within yourself and within the world, and you can do that quite simply by surrendering to divine will."

"Well," I said, "that sounds very similar to Buddhism, so it means believing something."

"No not really, all you have to do is surrender, you don't have to believe anything."

"Well you have to believe that surrendering is a good thing."

"Sure, but what have we got to surrender, really, when we are not talking about our wealth, loved ones, possessions, but surrendering to god. What have you got to surrender to god, really…?"

I paused and thought. "I guess the only thing I have to surrender is myself."

"Exactly. The only thing we all have to surrender is our minds, our hearts and our desires, the very things that stop us coming to god."

"But that is Buddhism, I objected, to let go of desires because they cause suffering."

"No, not to let go of desires, not to let go of anything, just to surrender to god. All the things we desire, all the people we love, this is the love of things or the other, but what I'm talking about here is a love greater than that, the love of god. If you do that you don't have to achieve anything else; if you surrender to god, because he created everything then you can trust he will look after everything, including you."

I was suspicious, was this an attempt to get me to join

something? Gabriel seemed like such a lovely man I could hardly believe that, but he was certainly warming to his subject.

"I don't mean god 'the Father'" – he made little quotation marks with the tips of his fingers as he said father – "who sits on a cloud, proud of his creation. The god I'm referring to has no form, no speech, no country, no color, no anything, he is simply the one source of everything. God is beyond all that, so to know him you have to get beyond all that too, so the only thing to do is to surrender yourself entirely; with your own mind and your own desires you will never be able to find God. To do that is everything, because then whatever comes to you is what god intends at that moment, so everything is just as it may be."

"It seems to me you are asking me to believe something."

"I'm not asking you to believe anything, in fact to believe nothing, just to experience surrender. What else is there really?"

"The will of God?"

"Yes, and that is all there is to surrender to, then you don't have to let go of desires to be enlightened, you in fact don't have to let go of anything, nor cling to anything, just surrender. Then the Divine Power brings you what is already in you. "

"Is this a teaching or religious belief or what?"

"No it is an experience. Really there cannot be a theory or a spiritual teaching for everyone because each person is different from another. Surrender and you get just what you need, just as if I surrender I get what I need."

"Did you make all this up?" I asked.

"Well, I discovered it for myself through the teachings of an enlightened being called Bapak, he made up Subud as a way of communicating what he learned when he had an instantaneous experience of surrender. But he is not a teacher or anything, quite the reverse, in fact he insists that all teachers are incorrect when they tell you to do something, or give you practices or anything like that. Usually a guru teaches his followers to do exactly the same as he does in order to reach what he has reached. But this is wrong, because each person is different and has to find his or her own way to divine surrender."

I was now intrigued. "So how do you go about surrendering?"

"You just do it, I couldn't show you how to do it but I can show you how I do it. I surrendered to your presence today, and now I am surrendering to these words, because that is my guidance right now. Then it's like all of a sudden everything stops, right now. My mind stops working and my heart stops working and my desires stop working, then because I am not looking for it or wanting it, I receive this gift."

He fell silent and I had nothing to say. I think I truly experienced the same inner silence he felt at that moment. Nothing to do, nothing to be, nothing to become, just breathing, just living, just being with my senses and my senses empty of all content. I don't know how long we sat there, but finally Gabriel broke the silence.

"Would you like another tea?" he asked in a matter-of-fact sort of way.

I was bemused. "What happened just then?"

"Nothing. Literally nothing, nothing replaced the something, the everything we are usually so busy with, in our minds, our emotions, our senses. That's all, Will. My inner experience is a matter between me and God, and no-one else can interfere, and it is the same for you. Tea?"

I declined the tea, and said I ought to leave. I felt I had to ask Gabriel why he was telling me this.

"You want the honest answer?"

"Of course."

"Pepper is going astray, what with his drugs and so on, that's bad enough, not because of the drugs per se, but because it leads him into all sorts of dangerous situations that disturb his equilibrium. On top of that he has got involved with an Indian Guru who teaches meditation but I've heard has sexual interest in his pupils. I just don't want you to go down the same track."

"But you don't even know me." I protested

Gabriel laughed. "But we are old friends," he joked, "you've been round here before." He paused. "Truth is, I don't know myself except through surrender. It is not about me knowing you, it is about you knowing you. But it is up to you, nothing is compulsory, everyone is free to come and go as they please, both here on earth and in their surrender to divine will."

"So, why are you telling me?"

"It just came to me. I was doing my latihan, that's what we call surrendering, and you came to the door. Strangely, I knew you because last time you came – when you knocked at the front door, I was in a similar state."

"Are you a follower of –what was his name - Batak?"

"He doesn't accept followers, that's the point. I was lucky enough to meet with him and travel quite extensively at one period, but as a companion not as a follower."

I felt challenging. "But you do this practice, he must have told you how to do it?"

"Not at all, there is nothing to tell, but he showed me what happened when he did it, just like I have shown you now. I don't know how you will do your latihan, but as you have experienced mine, then I know you will be able to do so as well."

He paused and looked deeply at me deeply. "Look Will, bottom line, whatever you think of what I'm saying, please be careful, don't go joining anything, don't believe someone else can show you, only you can show you what's inside you."

"That sounds wise," I admitted.

"I think it is the only wisdom."

*

Over the next couple of years, whenever I was in Cardiff I would go and visit Gabriel and have a shared latihan experience. I couldn't tell you much about it but in those early formative years after leaving home I think it was what saved me from getting involved in one or another of the gurus and such like that were proliferating at that time. Friends joined and tried to get me to join the Divine Light Mission with their boy guru; or to follow Swami S and his system of Transcendental Meditation; or to go to Nepal to meet Sri A., and so on. I always knew, because of my experience with Gabriel, that there truly is only one voice to listen to and that is the voice of divine will inside.

Of course after having these experiences with Gabriel, I read up on Subud and found pretty much what Gabriel had told me was accurate and true. According to Subud, whenever people try to find a way that may lead to contact with the divine, many become stranded on the path or, if not, are impelled to stray in other directions which are in reality only mirages of the imagination. By surrendering to something deeper inside oneself and silencing the mind and the imagination, we can make contact with God and learn to follow his divine will. They say that man's one and only way to be able to draw near to divine will is that he must be willing to quieten his inner feeling with complete patience, trust and sincerity. In truth, God can only be received in our hearts by those who have inner feelings filled with surrender, patience, trust and sincerity.

Pepper became deeply involved with the Divine Light Mission, and when he had a satsang meeting with the guru himself, he was thrown out for insulting the guru. Apparently the boy guru took a pipette and placed a drop of water onto his hand, saying this was like man before god; Pepper blew the water back up the guru's arm, saying that this is how we return to the source. Of course, Pepper's action had been quite creative and, using the guru's metaphor, quite accurate even, but to his followers what Pepper did was terrible. I tried to tell Pepper about Subud and get him to listen to his father, but I think the father-son dynamic was too strong for it to happen.

*

The last time I met Gabriel was at what could loosely be called an lsd party. By this time Pepper, still fearing the police, was living with me in my flat in Nottingham. One weekend a bunch of our mutual friends were visiting and on the Saturday afternoon many took a dose of lsd. There were so many people constantly arriving I didn't know who was invited or not but took the attitude the more the merrier. Usually if I took lsd I did so on my own or with one or two close friends, so it was quite unusual to be high whilst in a party atmosphere. I was quite shocked, however, entering the garden at the front of our flat to find Gabriel sitting on the grass apparently chatting up one of the young women there. Smiling broadly, he bade me sit next to him. After a short while, the young woman went off elsewhere and Gabriel turned to me in somewhat of a conspiratorial way and spoke softly.

"Have you taken acid like it seems everyone else here has?" he asked.

"Yes," I replied honestly. "Have you?"

"Oh dear, no," he replied. "Pepper had me try it once – well, it was good, just for exploration you understand." He paused. "But I prefer psilocybin myself."

I looked at him wide-eyed.

He laughed. "Just kidding," he said, beaming brightly. "Actually, yes I do prefer psilocybin, but my high of preference is my latihan." He looked around as if to check no one else was listening. "And you?" he asked.

I knew exactly what he meant and nodded assent. I admitted to him that although I still practiced surrendering to divine will, I found I could surrender more effectively by using lsd.

"Each to their own way, Will," said Gabriel acceptingly. He looked me up and down. "You don't look too bad on it." He laughed. "If I was your father, I guess I would want you to stop but truth is I can't get my own son to stop taking much worse things, so I'm hardly in a position to influence you."

I thought deeply about what he said. Finally, I spoke. "Gabriel, if you really thought it was best for me to stop, then I would do it. I respect your opinion very highly."

Gabriel was noticeably moved. He smiled. "Thank you, Will, that is lovely. Truth is, I know you will stop when you are ready. Trust that and you can't go wrong. But listen, when you do know that, you will surrender to it, yes?"

"Of course," I replied, and meant it. A couple of years passed before I reached that choice, but when I did Gabriel's advice was correct, I just stopped taking it because I knew I had taken enough. I had surrendered to its insights and charms, and effective clearing of much of my past conditioning, and knowing I didn't need it anymore surrendered to that instead.

Gabriel and I sat on the grass together a little while longer. "You'd better go party," he said, as people in all sorts of altered states joined us in the garden.

"It's not really my way," I said. "I prefer to look inside, for what the lsd shows me about myself and my inner workings."

"I know, but Will you have chosen to take it today at this party. All you have to do is surrender to that. Latihan never really stops, we just sometimes overlay it with other things and forget. Remember now."

We both laughed loud and long and soon a whole bunch of other people were lying on the grass with us, all laughing uncontrollably. I forgot Gabriel, or anyone else particularly, and entered into the spirit of the hippie party. It turned out to be one of the best trips of my life. By the time I thought of him again that day, Gabriel was nowhere to be found and I never met up with him again. When I asked Pepper where his dad was, he told me he wasn't there. I thought Pepper was just playing games with me, but he next day he insisted his father had not been there, in fact was quite adamant it was impossible, and he accused me of playing mind games with him. I knew I had seen and talked with Gabriel but just had to let it go. I thought I'd ask him next time I saw him, but as it turned out we never met again.

I eventually lost touch with them both as life moved on, but I rate Gabriel as one of the most amazing people I have met. An office worker, living an ordinary life and yet imbued with such an extraordinary perception of the world. Thank you, Gabriel, for saving me from teachers and gurus who have 'the truth', and guiding me towards understanding the true divine light which shines within.

Those moments of latihan, of surrendering to divine will, that I experienced with Gabriel were invaluable and helped put me in the right frame of mind to achieve the fullest advantage from the experiences I had with the other amazing people I was about to meet in my life. I most certainly would not have been ready for my meeting with Ashe.

5. Christianity with Ashe

Of all the amazing people who helped me find myself and my path in life, Ashe is the one I spent least time with, probably not more than two hours. I don't really recall when he visited my flat, but I know it was later the same evening as having seen the guru Sri A. speaking at a college in Derby. What a strange evening it was. A few friends and I had decided to drive to Derby to attend a lecture by Guru A. after we heard he had introduced meditation to intergovernmental bodies and actively worked for peace. To have the chance to see such an illustrious guru was compelling.

Guru A. glided into the room and took his place at the podium. For what seemed ages he didn't speak but appeared to be studying the audience which, being in a college, was mostly students. At some point I noticed he appeared to be looking at each person individually, so I paid very close attention to see if his eyes ever engaged mine. Even though I was expecting it, however, the impact of his gaze was somewhat shocking. For the moment of our contact I felt a warm, peaceful glow inside, as if Guru A. was looking into my soul.

I really liked his approach. He only spoke for a brief while and I do not remember the content of his address, but I think he was emphasising the importance of real relationship. Anyway, after his brief speech, he invited questions from the audience, saying that this was the way we could move into meaningful dialogue. I don't exactly know why, but I decided to ask him about prayer. I had been feeling rather depressed and, fearing a return of the depression from my teens, had started using my prayer formula once again. I wanted to hear what an Indian guru would have to say about this and how I might combine it with meditation. Of course I felt nervous to speak up in front of a room full of other students but Sri A.'s warm approach gave me confidence.

I barely heard the first couple of questions and answers, I was so busy trying to breathe calmly and prepare myself to stand and ask my question. My tummy was turning over and I felt more anxious than the situation seemed to really warrant. My time came, I was about to stand up to ask my question, when suddenly a short dark Asian man, who I had not even noticed before, shot to his feet and started a barrage of insults directed at Guru A.

"What are you doing here? Who do you think you are? We don't want your kind here! Go back to where you belong …" I do not really remember his exact words, of course, but he kept up this barrage of insults for less than a minute, then stormed out of the room.

My heart was beating fast and I certainly couldn't stand up and ask my question now. The effect the Asian man had had on me was astounding, but no more so than the effect his attack had on Guru A.

Clutching his forehead with both hands, Guru A. made a groan then sat down in his chair, his head held in his hands. There followed a difficult and rather embarrassing silence that seemed to last forever, then one of the organisers spoke softly to Guru A. words we in the audience couldn't hear. I presume he was asking Guru A. to continue but was answered in the negative. So, to all our surprise, the organiser announced that Guru A. was not feeling well and would not be taking any more questions. The guru glided out with his entourage, leaving the audience in an anti-climax. I think most of the students re-located to the bar, but for myself I felt too shocked by the event and decided to go home. My good friend George came with me.

Over the years, I've occasionally heard of Guru A. and

still wonder exactly what this episode was all about for him, and what if any lasting effect it had on him. That evening, however, my later meeting with Ashe was to change my life direction and give me an important understanding of my self and that there was more to Christianity than I had previously realised.

George and I had just made some coffee and were sitting in front of the electric fire when someone tapped lightly on the door. It was Lloyd, a Jamaican friend of ours with another guy I'd not seen before. George and Lloyd were quickly into rapping together, leaving the newcomer and myself to become acquainted.

He was in his mid to late twenties, had dark hair, bright dark eyes and a handsome Arabic face. He introduced himself as Ashe Ruff. He was Lebanese and visiting the U.K. only briefly. I didn't understand his name at first and had to ask him to repeat it. After several attempts he finally joked: "Well think of it this way. What a hippie doesn't want is rough hash, and I'm not rough hash I'm Ashe Ruff." We both laughed our heads off and his name was now firmly fixed in my mind.

At some point, Lloyd left and George fell asleep on one of the mattresses. Ashe was sitting close to me and we were talking quite intimately about the meaning of life, what we understood about politics and so on. I felt very relaxed in his presence. He told me, I remember, that all Lebanese people, like himself, were traders at heart but, although he had traded – and smuggled – many items, he preferred mostly to trade in wisdom and understanding. In fact he said the phrase wisdom and understanding several times and it was only in later years, after I discovered Kabbalah, that I understood he was referring to the Supernal Triad and the essential qualities of the Creator.

Ashe was regaling me with a potted history of the Lebanon. I previously had no knowledge of the Muslim and

Christian factions in his country and found his descriptions of the enmity between them very interesting, if somewhat frightening. At some point in the discussion, Ashe referred again to the theme of trading in wisdom and understanding and asked me if I would like to trade with him.

"I don't think I have any wisdom and understanding to trade," I hastily responded.

"Of course you do," he countered. "No one can reach your age without already having a vast store of understanding even if you are still short on wisdom." He laughed. "You just don't recognise it in yourself. Think carefully, there must be something."

What came to my mind was my formula for prayer and how it had lifted me out of my teenage depression. I had planned to ask Guru A. about this, so it seemed something to bring to 'trade' with Ashe. I didn't really think what I was trading was worth much, but I shared with him anyway.

I told Ashe that during the period of my worst depression in my teens, every night before sleep, and in the morning upon waking, I followed a simple prayer regime. Making myself as peaceful as possible, I praised God, said I was sorry for all I had done wrong, thanked God for all the good things in my life, and then I asked for the cloud to be lifted away. I added that I did not think faith was a vital part of the process because even when praying to 'God' I hadn't really believed in his (or her, or its) existence.

Ashe asked me to repeat the essential features of the prayer formula I had created.

"Well," I replied, "it always felt vital to be still, to make myself as peaceful as possible. Then I praised God, apologised for anything I had done wrong, thanked God for all the good things in my life, and then I asked for the cloud to be lifted away."

When I had finished, Ashe was silent for a considerable time before he finally spoke. "You are talking about pacts," he simply said.

I told him I had no idea what he was talking about.

"Pacts. You make pacts with the Lord."

I thought I understood. "Oh pax, peace, to make peace with God," I said.

"No, no, not pax, pacts – it is an acronym, listen P.A.C.T.S., pacts."

"I still don't get it."

"P is for peace, A is for Adoration, C is for Confession, T is for Thanksgiving, S is for Supplication. Bring yourself to peace – P; praise god, adoration – A; thank god, thanksgiving - T; ask for what you want, supplication – S."

I must have still looked somewhat nonplussed.

"Just like your prayer," Ashe said emphatically.

This time it went in, and really deeply. Ashe had made a formula out of the form of prayer I had invented. I was amazed.

"No, listen, I haven't made a formula out of your form," he said sharply. "You tuned into a universal formula for prayer, you discovered pacts for yourself. Neither you nor I made it up, the Creator did."

I was quite speechless; could this be really true?

"I expect you sometimes secretly thought you were Jesus, Will," he said softly.

I had never told anyone this, not admitted it even to myself, it seemed such a blasphemous and shaming thought, but now I freely admitted this to Ashe. It was a liberating disclosure. I felt like I was breathing again.

"Will, there is nothing to be ashamed of, it just shows how well you were making your pacts with the Lord. There is a hidden path in Christianity that keeps the true flame alight. Of course, you are Jesus." he paused for a moment. "And so am I, so is everyone because Jesus is in all our hearts. Well, not really Jesus, because he was a man like us, albeit a special one. What is in our hearts, all our hearts, is the Lord."

"But isn't Jesus the Lord?" I asked.

"No, Jesus embodied the Lord more fully than anyone had ever done before him, he was truly the Son of God in being able to do so, but what is important to us is that he was also, as he said himself, the Son of Man."

I didn't fully understand so Ashe explained further. "If Jesus had just been the Son of God then it would be no miracle that he embodied the Lord, or resurrected in his light body after his physical death. The fact that he was the Son of Man, like you, me and the rest of us, is what makes his life so exemplary for us. If he could do it, as he showed us, then – at least potentially – we all can do it."

I must have appeared sceptical and mumbled something to that effect. "The point is, Will, that to be sceptical is correct, you are not really able to believe in something you have not experienced. But think of it, you have experienced the power of making pacts with the Lord, so you do know."

"But that doesn't make me enlightened like Jesus," I protested.

"No, not in your everyday Self, you are right, not at all. But you, like me, are in the Lord and can experience the Lord supporting you through your life."

"How?"

"The Lord isn't Jesus, or a person, the Lord is a special energy we can experience when we silence ourselves. It is as if everything – and I mean absolutely everything – that we experience in life is, say, this table" – he pointed to a small coffee table in the middle of my room – "and we think it is everything there is, but really it is like this table in this room, if you can relax your gaze and silence yourself, you can experience the table isn't everything, it is just one table, one quite small object, in a relatively large room."

"And the table is everything?"

"Everything"

"Then it must include Jesus too."

"Yes, it includes Jesus. The only thing it doesn't include is the Lord and of course once we give the Lord a name it becomes a thing on the table. The Lord is a name for - shall I call it something? – the vast unknown, pregnant with all potential, that surrounds, interpenetrates, permeates all that exists and is always more than anything and everything."

I think he was losing me a little as his explanation became more complex, and obtuse. Recognising this, Ashe spoke firmly.

"Will, I offered you a trade. Would you like our exchange trade to be fulfilled now?"

"Of course," I said, not really knowing what he meant. Then in the following few moments I had a full and lasting experience of the Lord.

*

What can I tell you about that experience except to say I came to it through my heart, through experiencing a deep level of forgiveness for everything I had ever done wrong and for everyone else's mistakes, and it transcended everything I could or ever could experience. That's why I cannot tell you anything about it because anything I say about it isn't it, at best can only be words describing something that is not only beyond words, it is beyond definition to give it words. I sometimes think when people have deep conversion experiences and talk about Jesus being in their hearts, guiding them, that they may be describing the same thing. I don't know, though, because for me to say Jesus was in my heart, as lovely an image as that is, it still doesn't even come close to experiencing the Lord.

Ashe left soon after and I never met him again, I suppose he returned to the Lebanon and after that, who knows? But my trade with Ashe was a tremendous milestone in my life that has underpinned all my experiences of wisdom and understanding since.

There is a rider to this story, too. I always remembered Ashe Ruff's name, of course, but had never connected it with anything else. Indeed, the joke about rough hash, whilst making the name memorable, also had the effect of reducing his name to the absurd rather than elevating it in any way.

One of the things that had led me to my experience of the Lord was Ashe's insistence that forgiveness is the key to all enlightenment. He quoted Jesus as saying 'Forgive them Lord, for they know not what they do' as being the key to being able to understand how Jesus was able to withstand the pain of the crucifixion and attain to the fully enlightened state. This made sense to me for I already knew that forgiveness, like for instance turning the other cheek, is a very powerful tool. But it was more than thirty years later that I received the final key to understanding the significance of Ashe's presence in my life.

My partner and I made a trip to California in the late 1990s and I bought a pile of CDs. One of them was by Steve Shehan and Basly Othmani, a record titled 'Assarouf'. I loved the album and played it regularly for a number of years, literally dozens of times. One day, looking at the back cover, I saw that under the title Assarouf it had, in small letters in brackets, 'forgiveness'. Finally, all these years later, I had understood Ashe's real name – it wasn't Ashe Ruff at all, it was Assarouf.

6. Shamanism with Tomas

The more I reflected on Anandapuran's task that I should remember the seven most amazing people I had met, the easier it became. Justin, Seamus, Gabriel and Ashe were obvious choices, although they hadn't necessarily sprung to mind immediately. I was curious to discover though that I had met amazing people and yet not really taken in at the time either how amazing they were nor the effect they had on my life.

I was reflecting yet again on all this one day and felt quite despondent. I'd had several lovely girl-friends who were quite amazing in themselves. They could be the subject of a different quest, but I just knew that none of them constituted the amazing people Anandapuran had set me to remember. I had several interesting friends, some of whom I loved dearly, but they also were not the people I was trying to remember. I was working hard at trying to remember everyone I had ever met but not really getting anywhere. Mostly it seemed they were people who had made relatively brief appearances in my life – well, in fact, sometimes very brief indeed – but had momentous effect, not unlike Anandapuran himself.

There were two people who there was no choice about, though, as they had the most profound and lasting effect on me. The first of these was Tomas. He had been brought up in Norway although his father was a jazz musician who was apparently half Mexican, and who was a colleague of the famous musician Don Cherry who also had children who grew up in Scandinavia. Tomas's mother was Spanish but had ended up living in Norway bringing up Tomas and his two sisters. At least, that was what Tomas told me but he may have been disguising his past.

I'd previously met Tomas through a mutual friend called Mike. Tomas was a really very beautiful man who, with his dark complexion, long straight dark hair and bony face structure, looked like the archetypal American Indian. He'd led a really interesting life, travelling part of the time with his jazz musician father around the world, but mostly in the States, and living part of the time with his mother who spent half the year in Norway and half in Spain with her parents. The relationship between Tomas's parents was obviously very fiery, but it didn't appear to have caused him any great trauma as a child and indeed he was the most genuinely 'cool' person I ever met.

Tomas was originally Mike's friend but whenever we had met up, which was probably only three or four times, we had a strong rapport. At the time, in my early twenties, I wasn't feeling very confident in my life and I found it hard to believe that someone as tuned in as Tomas could really like me, let alone respect me, but all the signals suggested he did. He had even asked if he could call to see me at my flat the next time he was in town and of course I had agreed, but I never really thought he would do so, so wasn't really ever expecting him.

On the night of Tomas's visit, Pepper was staying at my flat and we had taken a small dose of lsd together. We weren't having a very good trip, the lsd wasn't really strong enough and we were caught in a strange limbo space where everything was different but not different enough. I think we both felt rather bored in fact, although I don't think we could have admitted that to one another at the time. Somehow we ended up playing cards which seemed a strange thing to do whilst on a trip, but I think we were just trying to pass the time until the drug wore off. Mind you, it wasn't all bad, and there was something quite surreal in the way the cards came up and we both found we could apparently predict which cards would come next, which added a strange dimension to gin rummy. Sometimes even now, more than forty years later, I still get memories of this whilst playing rummy, and, believe it or not, still sometimes find I can predict which cards are going to emerge from the blind pack, or apparently influence which card the other players will choose to throw away. Anyway, I convince myself that's true!

As Pepper and I were playing gin rummy for little other reason than to pass away the time, I was quite glad when the doorbell rang and hoped we might be stimulated by someone else's presence. Well, I was delighted and surprised by who had arrived; I had no idea who she was, but she was the most beautiful brunette I had ever seen. Remember I was under the influence of lsd so I never asked her name, just languidly invited her in. Pepper was as amazed by this beautiful woman as me. She sat on the floor next to us and proceeded to prepare a chillum of grass for us to smoke. A chillum was a popular smoking device used by hippies at that time, consisting of a clay tube, wider at one end (into which the smoking mixture was inserted) and narrower at the other end (through which it was smoked.) Actually chillums were pretty awful, usually causing the smokers to cough endlessly. Everyone at the time pretended it was great, though, and, rather strangely, the coughing fits were seen as part of the process!

I couldn't stop staring at this beautiful woman, she was astonishingly pretty. Her large eyes were like big clear pools of deep blue water; her lips were full and deep red and she had a habit of sticking her tongue a small way out as she concentrated on preparing the chillum. The whole thing was so erotic I started to feel really embarrassed with the physical effect she was having on me. I couldn't really look away, however, and when I glanced at Pepper I could see she was having the same effect on him.

We hardly spoke at all but that wasn't unusual in those hippie days when we sat round stoned. I think my dose of lsd might have kicked in stronger I'm not sure, but it felt like she took absolutely ages over packing the chillum, not that I minded, I was entering in and out of a timeless space in which all I could do was marvel at her beauty, and eroticising energy.

Finally, the chillum was ready and she started to perform a ritual with it that I had not seen before. Usually once a chillum or joint was ready it would be lit and passed round. Occasionally the roller would pass it to someone else to light up first, and that was as close as we got to anything like a conscious ritual. With this woman, though, everything was done slowly and deliberately, and with deep feeling. She seemed to understand that Pepper and I weren't used to smoking in this way and she explained what she was doing to us.

"I call this the ritual of our sister Maria Jane," she said. "Marijuana, you know."

I think both Pepper and I must have looked truly impressed. I felt like we were being let in on a secret. I probably had, but at that moment, I thought I had never realised that marijuana was Mary Jane.

"The sacrament comes in three forms," she continued. "The black which is the monthly blood of Maria, the gold which is the milk from her breasts, and the green, as we have tonight, which enables us to partake of our mother's aura."

Now she was losing me, but I listened intently. Her words sounded as beautiful as she looked.

"Look at the chillum," she continued. "The bowl is the sphere of heaven. The mixture I am putting inside is the grace of the goddess. The fire we will apply to light it is her creative desire towards us. The water droplets in our breath as we take it in purifies the soul ready for the union. The smoke is the perfume of the goddess herself. The tube through which it passes is the influence from within. The mouthpiece is the love of a divine kiss."

She paused for a moment before continuing, lovingly holding the chillum before her, now ready to use. "The inhalation brings enlightenment to the soul." She held the chillum momentarily before her forehead then, bringing it to her lips, ignited the mixture and breathed in. After holding her breath for moments, she breathed out, saying: "The exhalation is the influence shed upon fellow travellers."

Not immediately passing the chillum on, which would be the usual custom, she seemed to ponder deeply for a few moments then continued. "Maria, she is the goddess of the leaves, our little sister. She is alluring, seductive, she controls time, she slows time, she stops time .... she opens the spaces between moments, she has the sweetest of scents. She brings spontaneity, humour, love, sensitivity, and awareness of her plane of existence. Do you understand?"

Pepper and I both nodded, eager to have our turn on this now powerfully charged chillum. Our new friend took another toke, before passing it on, a long slow toke that seemed to light up her face. "Ah, Maria," she sighed as she passed me the chillum for the first time. "She intoxicates the senses. Her smell is that of perspiration and sex; her taste is of skin, salt, saliva, sexual fluids; her sight is a light in the eyes; her sound is like a heartbeat, breathing, gurgling, sucking, and her touch – feel the chillum in your hands now – her touch is the temple for your tongue."

I quickly put the chillum to my forehead, taking my cue from how she had done it, and took a puff on the mix before passing it on to Pepper. He followed suit and passed the chillum reverentially back to this woman who took it from him as if she was taking a delicate new born baby to cradle.

Well, I'm not sure if either Pepper or I had more than one toke on the chillum, but the mysterious woman blew such large amounts with each toke, it quickly burnt away. This was the early seventies and, certainly for us hippies in England at the time, this was 'pre-feminist' days. I don't think we were in any way intentionally sexist, but that was the culture we were still operating within. So to be sitting, whilst under the influence of a mind-altering drug, with such a powerful woman who spoke openly with such strong erotic feeling, was quite mind blowing. I was both unbelievably attracted to her and terrified at the same time. She was so powerful she held both Pepper and I enraptured simply by her presence. Apart from her ritual, nothing else was spoken between us. I remember at one point looking deeply into her eyes for what seemed liked ages and experiencing an endless orgasm of sheer delight. She met my gaze and held it without any sense of inhibition. We weren't even touching, but I felt like we were making love in the most satisfying and exciting way possible. It was as if every sinew in her body directed her flesh towards me and pulled me into her, so I penetrated not her sexual organs but her whole being. Then at the point of orgasm she would hold me hovering on the brink of the deepest chasm of sheer delight. Of course, I'm using words here to try to describe an experience that was wonderfully and truly erotic and beyond adequate description.

What became clearer and clearer as time slowly passed was that the mysterious woman had complete control over both Pepper and me. We were like putty in her fingers, she could have done whatever she liked with us. Her visage kept changing too, so sometimes she looked like a fair Scandinavian woman, then she would become a dark, sultry Spanish woman, then an Amerindian Chief proud and strong, then a slinky and sexy black woman, then a black man, then …I suddenly realised who she was.

"Tomas," I said tentatively.

"Yes, Will," he replied.

"It is you, isn't it? Tomas it's you!"

"Of course," he replied matter-of-factly. "Who did you think I was?"

How could I answer that? In my mind he had been a thousand different amazing people but mostly this weirdly erotic woman of immense power.

Pepper looked confused and I tried to introduce him to Tomas but he was completely disorientated. I guess the shock for him of finding this person was not a woman but also that he was a friend of mine was just too much for him to take in. He explained that he just had to go and lie down. I tried to make sure he was okay but he brushed off my concerns and said he was fine, he just needed be alone, and departed to his bedroom.

Tomas and I were alone. I felt more than a little embarrassed when I remembered how I had been erotically exchanging with him a few moments before. What would he think of me and how I had been behaving? He didn't know that Pepper and I had taken lsd so I did not even have that as an excuse. I think I tried to mutter something about it, but I needn't have worried, Tomas understood a lot more than I realised.

"I learned to focus in that way from an Indian shaman that my father had taken me to see when we were touring in California," he explained. "It's very hot, isn't it? It always makes me feel like I'm having super sex." He laughed freely.

"I thought you were a woman," I admitted.

"Sometimes I am," he countered, laughing even more. "The shaman showed me that we all have a double, it's really beyond gender, but it tends to take the form of the opposite gender to whatever we are, so as a man my double takes the form of a woman."

"Do I have a double?" I asked.

"We all do ... and I'll tell you something, Will. When you thought I was a woman, I was seeing you as one too. " He laughed. "We must have looked like a pair of lesbians!"

I felt more relaxed and asked Tomas to tell me more about the shaman he had met. I'd always been interested in the 'medicine men' in cowboy movies and had gathered that the person Tomas referred to was a genuine medicine man.

"Oh yes, he was," Tomas said. I noticed a tone of reverence, or maybe even gratefulness, come into his voice. "He showed me how to work with energy, to make it move."

What do you mean?"

"Well, look at this." So saying, Tomas fixed my gaze and we looked deep into one another's eyes. Then he made a sound, like 'hooo', and as he spoke instead of hearing the sound of 'hooo' I saw it come out of his mouth like multi-coloured blocks cut into the shape of the letters that represent the sound he was making.

"Of course" he said, speaking normally now, "you might not usually be able to see that, it is the drug that has opened you to seeing it" - Tomas had easily deduced I was under the influence of a psychotropic drug - "but the shaman and his people could turn on that faculty without taking any drugs, and he told me how to."

"Can you show me?" I asked.

"It's not about doing a specific trick, though. It requires you to work at it daily, to live your life by a certain set of principles.

To clear out all the old conditioning that keeps the world as you usually see it, and to make the space to see the world in a completely new way."

I've no idea what time it was when we started talking, probably quite late, but it was well after dawn by the time Tomas had finished sharing with me something of what he had learned from the shaman he had met.

"The basic premise is that the so-called reality of our ordinary world is just a story we tell ourselves to make it real, but it isn't really so. Do you understand this?"

"I'm tripping, Tomas," I replied.

"Yes," he responded, slightly tremulously, "but it has to be without drugs of any kind, even enhancing ones like lsd. I mean even in non-altered states of reality you have to become aware that everything isn't always as it seems, in fact is never as it seems." I nodded eagerly, I knew this well already.

"So this story we tell ourselves keeps the world we usually inhabit in place, as it were. It's one description of many possible different ones we could use to describe what's really out there, so to speak. We have developed it over many aeons, though, and it serves us well – so long as we remember it is a description and not the real thing itself."

Tomas paused and sipped slowly from the glass of water I had fetched him earlier. He appeared to be searching for the right words and the wait seemed interminable to me. I had to hold back from telling him to go on as I was so eager to hear more. "It is possible to turn off this reality and see the world as it really is, or perhaps more correctly, to see the world from different perspectives. Shamans call it 'seeing', as opposed to what we habitually do which is just look."

"Like when I saw the words you were speaking?" I asked.

"Yes, and more than that, to not put another illusionary description on it, so not to believe you don't see words, or to see words, but to just see the energy."

"How can I see energy?"

"Better said is how can you not see energy. You are seeing it now, the point is to stop describing it to yourself as one thing or another, and just be with the experience."

We both fell silent for a while. I was trying to do what Tomas had said but nothing seemed to change. Tomas seemed to understand what I was trying to do.

"Stop trying," he continued, "because trying gets in the way. Just do it. Do what? Well, to just do it, as it were, there are some necessary preliminary steps, and you can't just believe they will lead to success because any such belief will cause it to fail. You just have to do it." He smiled widely at me, his big infectious grin. Momentarily he looked once more like the beautiful woman I'd seen earlier. I felt a stirring of passion.

"That's it," he said jubilantly. "For a moment you saw, and your body responded. Of course, you experienced it in a particular way that is held in place by all your conditioning and imprinting through your life – so I was a beautiful woman, you felt a surge of desire, you repressed it because it didn't feel right, and so on. This is your personal history, or so shamans call it, and a necessary first step towards seeing is to eradicate your personal history. All we know of ourselves, all that others know of us, is this history that keeps us held in the consensus reality we are trying to move away from. It is a hook that keeps us caught up in the set conditioning presented to us as children. Equally it is the hook whereby others help – unwittingly for they are equally hooked – to keep us in place. Indeed personal history is not so much what we know but what is known of us by others. If we erase this history we are free from the conceptions others have of us, and which entrap us in an identity we have not chosen."

Tomas paused and looked at me deeply. "Think of it Will, what do you know of me?"

Actually I realised I knew very little. "Well, "I started, " you are –"

Tomas interrupted me. "No, I'm not. That is just a description of me you've built up, but it isn't me."

"You are Mike's friend," I said.

"No I'm not. I do friendship with Mike, and you too now, but that's not who I am."

"You're a man who was born in Spain and lived in Norway."

"Who told you that? How do you know it is true? And even if factually it is true does it tell you who I am?"

I admitted it, I didn't know who he was at all!

"But you can see me now. See me," he commanded.

Nothing happened, he was still the same Tomas.

"Of course I am still Tomas – and that's not me anymore than 'Will' is you."

Then we're not really here," I said jokingly.

Tomas kicked me. "We most certainly are here," he said, laughing. Sweeping his hands in a broad gesture to indicate everything else: "It's all this that's not really here!"

"Listen, as we start to erase our personal history we must become inaccessible to the world at large, we must stop bolstering our ego's idea of ourselves, our self importance, for it is this which stops us seeing the world as it is. So long as we are self important ego, we are separate, and such separation precludes any chance we might have of understanding either our inner or outer perceptions."

Tomas stopped suddenly and looked at me with apparent alarm. "Will, you are going to die!" he exclaimed very loudly.

My heart jolted, my hairs stood on end. "What?"

"You are going to die!" Tomas exclaimed again.

"Um, no I'm not, not just now, I don't think so," I rather meekly replied, not sure whether he was right or I was. I felt quite frightened.

"Truth is, you have no way of knowing whether this moment – or this moment, or this moment, or any moment, is going to be your last. If you allow death to be with you, to stalk you in this way, how can you feel more, or less, important than anything else. How can we miss the importance of any moment? It is not enough to intellectually understand this, you have to live with it, to live with death always there waiting for you, then you will choose to make the best of each and every moment."

That made complete sense. "Be here now," I said.

"Yes, exactly. Be. Here. Now. Seeing is just that, when you are being here now you are truly seeing, not just looking. There's no time for superficially looking when this moment is your last." He paused. "Last moment: what to do now then?"

"Have a cup of tea!" I replied, half jokingly.

Tomas almost doubled over with laughter. "Said like a true Englishman, " he cried. "But also like a true shaman, my shaman would have loved your answer because bottom line is what else is there to do but have a cup of tea?"

We sat silently. I was deeply moved.

"Go on, then," Tomas finally said.

It broke my reverie. "Go on what?" I asked.

"Make some tea of course!"

*

The first rays of dawn were showing in the sky as Tomas and I silently sipped the tea I had brewed. I'd been to check on Pepper but he was fast asleep, and snoring. Tomas and I were now sitting, instead of on the floor in my room, in the kitchen on two old dining table chairs, pulled up to the window. A cold presence crept through the window, but the sky was magnificent. The birds had started a rich dawn chorus to which I rapturously listened. I was trying to see the world, as Tomas had described, and felt I was perhaps starting to understand him.

One particularly loud song came from a blackbird sitting on a branch of the old walnut tree in the back yard. I'd heard this bird before, it was there singing every morning and this was not the first time I'd been sitting in this window looking at the dawn rising. Tomas's attention had also been attracted by the blackbird.

"You can hear that blackbird every morning, singing his song regularly," he said. I nodded assent. "And so," continued Tomas, "if you wanted to catch and eat that blackbird you'd know where and when to find him"

I was shocked by his words. "But I love the bird and wouldn't want to harm it," I objected.

"Neither would I, Will. But what I said is true nevertheless. If we wanted to we'd know where and when to trap him, yes?"

I had to agree.

"That's because of his personal history and his habitual acts. It is the same for us. If some force wanted to capture and eat you, it would be easy. It could watch you for a few days, learn your routines and then it would be easy to trap you. We have to learn to disrupt our life routines, it is a major part of stopping creating personal history. Our routines make us accessible. If you wish to remain free, untrapped, unhooked by ordinary reality, you must leave no trail of routines which may be hunted."

Tomas kept pausing, as if giving me time to take in what he was saying. "But as well as being inaccessible regarding your personal history, you at the same time need to make yourself accessible to power. Routines lead to annihilation; power brings freedom. To be accessible to power we have to be aware of our actions and realise our true intent. Learning this though is not enough, to act upon it is necessary. Power is the major concern of a shaman, not power over others, though that may sometimes be part if it, but power as the flow, the intent of life.

"There is no use in the shaman's world for sadness, remorse or complaints. No 'poor baby me' stuff allowed here. You have to assume full responsibility for you yourself. And in this responsible life, somewhat paradoxically, you also have to let go, surrender, abandon yourself. No time for asking why. Life is a constant challenge, not between good and bad or any other such dualities, but between taking or not taking the challenge which is always just a challenge and nothing more. This way you store power and power brings the ability to stop the old world and see, just see. Each time you follow intent, whether that is to say yes or no to the challenge, you store power; every time you go against intent, you lose power. Now before you ask what intent is, I can tell you I cannot answer that because any answer I might give wouldn't be really the answer. Intent is something that comes from other realms, it can guide us, but it is impersonal and it is our task to engage with it impersonally and follow it where it leads us."

I was feeling tired. "I think I understand," I said, "but how can I do this practically, what can I do to wake up as it were, to become a shaman as you are describing it, it is abstract."

"The shaman's knowledge is abstract, my friend, that is what gives it power. But at a concrete level, there are practices.

Look at the shadows of things rather than at the things themselves; look at the spaces between the leaves on a tree rather than at the leaves; such practices help you shift your attention which is a necessary step to seeing.

"You can transform your world in this way, through shifts of the eyes, creating double vision by crossing the eyes, by gazing, staring, blinking, and so on. In a sense this fools the mind, but really it only fools that part of the mind which keeps the 'illusion out there' static instead of letting us see the true fluidity of nature. Ultimately you have to shift your gaze, your attention you give to yourself in the same way, defeating the illusion in there" – Tomas pointed at my chest – "which stops you being fully in your power. All doing is partial and the only real thing in your being is that you are going to die. "

"And then?" I asked.

"You shift your perceptions and find yourself in a dimension which will alter and transform itself according to your intent. Indeed, you will realise that the essence of shamanism is in fact transformation, an unquestionable fact."

Tomas yawned, long and deep. I don't think I'd ever seen anyone yawn so widely. I was transfixed. As he finished his yawn he suddenly let out a loud piercing yelp. I nearly jumped out of my skin, and for a moment my perception changed. It wasn't the drug anymore, I truly felt something inside me change and momentarily I saw the world. I was no longer looking, I was seeing. I didn't have to look at the spaces between the leaves, or hear the silence between sounds, for all such distinctions became at best arbitrary and at worst limiting.

"Yes," said Tomas. "That's it, my friend. Let's go snooze."

*

By the time I woke up sometime during the middle of the afternoon, I discovered Tomas had left. I felt really disappointed, and could hardly remember all he had shared with me about the path of shamanism. I was sitting sipping from a cup of coffee trying my hardest to recall the instructions he had given me for seeing rather than looking. Pepper, who had risen about the same time as me, was full of how strange it was we had mistaken Tomas for a woman, and a beautiful woman at that, but I wasn't really interested in this. Tomas had whetted my appetite for the teachings he had received and I couldn't – didn't want to – break my concentration in trying to remember stuff. I was glad that Pepper was also leaving that afternoon and after he left I felt glad to be alone. That feeling didn't last long, though, as very quickly I felt a depressive mood coming on and became very lonely. I remember sitting disconsolately in one of the chairs in the kitchen, looking out of the window most definitely not succeeding in seeing the spaces between the leaves.

When the door bell rang I was up like a shot, glad of the company of whoever was there. I was then doubly delighted to see it was Tomas, looking fresh and awake and carrying a large bag of shopping.

"One of the most important things my shaman told me," he explained as we entered the kitchen and he emptied his bag of fresh vegetables onto the table, "perhaps the most important thing, is that we eat well. Fresh and wholegrain, that's the key. It is so easy, particularly for us young people, to grab foods that are instant and not really nourishing. So I thought I'd make us a wholesome dinner. You on for helping?"

Of course I was. I already did some cooking, I wasn't totally helpless in that department, but that afternoon Tomas helped me to realise just how satisfying it was to unhurriedly prepare fresh vegetables and fruits into a quality meal. He showed me how to dice several carrots at once (he had apparently worked in a restaurant at some point), how to reduce a stock, how to lightly braise items to make them tastier, and so on. Mostly however he showed me how to make each step in the preparing and cooking of food into a meditative act, to enjoy the process and not be attached to the final outcome. It was a real eye-opener for me and, as we worked on our meal, Tomas told me more about the shamanic teachings he had received.

"One of the ways we maintain the structure of our world and believe it to be the whole truth is through constantly talking to ourselves about it," Tomas explained. "We have an inner dialogue with ourselves – as if we are not one but a multitude of beings." He laughed.

I knew exactly what he meant. Just that afternoon when I had been trying to see the trees again, I had felt annoyed with myself for constantly telling myself how to do it, another voice telling me I was doing it wrong, another voice telling me to give up, it was meaningless, another voice telling me to go do something else, and so on. I told Tomas of this, and how I had literally shouted 'Shut Up!' to these voices.

"Exactly. And shouting shut up, so long as you do it out loud and clearly, is a good shamanic technique. You just have to notice the space directly after you shout shut up and enter into it, before they all start chattering again."

"The space?" I asked. "What do you mean?"

"At the heart of shamanic work is the necessity to learn to turn off your inner dialogue. Indeed, that's not particular to shamanism, the state where the internal dialogue is stopped is well known in all spiritual traditions and transcendent religions. In Hindu terminology it is called dhyana, for instance, my father used to work with that. It is the root of the word zen, you know. Zen meditation may be explained as a form of meditation aimed at turning off the internal dialogue. Even the little zen stories about the sound of one hand clapping and so on, they have the same aim."

"Inner peace?" I suggested. I thought of Gabriel and the peace I had learned to connect with through laitihan.

"Yes, that's the first part. The internal dialogue is what grounds us, the world is such and such, is the way it is because we talk to ourselves about it being that way. To stop the internal dialogue is the only way of stopping the regular world view and entering into the world of shamans.

"When you really shut up, the everyday, ordinary world doesn't hold up anymore and the space created opens us up to extraordinary aspects of ourselves. In that space any intent we hold is made true whether the intent is relating to action in this world, which we inevitably re-enter, or to do with the other worlds we access then."

I needed him to explain further.

"My shaman taught me that any thought we hold in the state of complete inner silence becomes a command, really because there are no thoughts to compete with it. When you learn to stop the internal dialogue everything becomes possible. You could say the world adjusts itself to itself."

I really didn't understand that but Tomas explained that some things are just simply beyond explanation. "You have to experience it and that requires you to continue working on it. You'll know when you are starting to make progress because you'll notice more synchronicities. You know what they are?"

I had read some of the writings of Carl Jung and told Tomas I did. "Co-incidences that mean something to the observer," I suggested.

"Well, yes," he replied, "sort of. It is just that they are there all the time because everything is really connected anyway, we just miss it. Or when we experience this level of connection the ordinary world-view is to treat it as co-incidence, that is reasonable, that's what reason wants to do with that experience. To uphold its own singular point of view, to support ego in thinking it is it. But as we work on stopping the internal dialogue these incidents increase and we can see – and I mean see here, truly see – that these 'coincidences' are not that at all, they are not anything to do with reason, they are the manifestation of intent. A synchronicity, it's a good word for it, a synchronicity is the way intent sees the world."

We continued chopping vegetables in silence. Tomas was adding some of them to a pot, ready to make a stew, whilst others went straight onto the plate, he explaining that if we have half of our food raw it helps the body digest food and not treat it as poison to the system. The idea of food being poison seemed strange to me but Tomas told me that all cooked food has that kind of effect which is why we should always eat something raw first before eating cooked food. I was thinking about this and, I suppose having an internal dialogue with myself about it, when Tomas suddenly returned to the subject of shamanism.

"The ego is the organiser of the world, trying to make everything make sense and everyone see reason – its own reason. It attempts to take the chaos that we live in and turn it into something familiar and safe and then hold it like that. It is intended to be our servant, a guardian even, by helping us to function in the world and putting meaning into things. Problem is, as it is truly then everything we are, we think that it is everything there is." He paused for his words to sink in.

"We have a description of the world which we are taught from when we are born and we go on substantiating and adding to as we age. We take it for granted. It begins at birth and it ends at death; it has no continuance. Truth is, though, it is only a very small part of us, for there is a greater, infinite part of us that cannot be named because once we try to name it, ego grabs it and adds it into its world."

"Then it must be impossible to talk about it," I suggested. I told Tomas about Ashe and the way he had named the infinite part of us 'the lord' and used the analogy that everything we could know being like a table in a large room, and the lord being the rest of the room that we forget exists, believing the table to be everything.

"Indeed. But the infinite cannot be conceptualised in any way, not as a table or a room, not anything. It's the Tao that cannot be named. But, and this is our saving grace, as it were, it can be witnessed. It is beyond all duality and a shaman reaches the state where he can witness this alternate reality, this underlying true reality we might even say, through..."

I interrupted him. "Don't tell me, I know – through stopping the internal dialogue."

"Exactly!"

I think I really understood what he was saying but still felt this was too difficult a task, I needed more practical advice. Tomas understood this but refrained from responding to my querying looks. We worked together quietly and, as the vegetable stew was now cooking, and the raw vegetables were all ready, I made some tea and we sat before the window once again. It was early evening and the sky had darkened, large rain clouds looming ahead, a sprinkle of wet already obscuring the view of the tree outside.

Tomas sounded sad when he spoke. "That's all there is really," he said, "raindrops on a window."

His words, or maybe it was his sadness, but something just then had a profound effect on me. It was as if I became aware of the other world that underlies our apparent world. I felt a deep moving sadness too, not because anything was wrong, but more because of a sense of profound incompleteness. I felt as if I were inside an echo chamber, and everything outside echoed in this chamber and was unreal. It was such an intense experience I became very frightened and started to panic. Tomas muttered some soothing words, however, and I started to relax. Then suddenly the tree outside lit up, maybe it was the last rays of the setting sun breaking through the cloud, I don't know, and I don't think I will ever know. The tree outside the window simply lit up. I felt a sense of great lucidity, I felt an almost dream-like detachment yet completely engaged at the same time. Everything became crystal clear.

Tomas and I ate the delicious meal we had prepared and he promised me that we would be friends always, even if we never met again. He left later in the evening and in fact I have not seen him since. Shortly after this time, I moved and it wasn't that long before I met Marie and started my new life as a 'married man' (albeit a very hippie-like version of such). I guess I thought of Tomas but having no address for him I couldn't tell him of my move. Maybe I trusted that he would find where I lived, or maybe I just trusted that somehow we would meet again, when intent made it so. However it happened, I lost touch with not only the man himself, but strange though it seems to me, I even spent long periods of my life not realising how significant this time we had spent together was in my life.

As I write this now, I realise that Tomas was one of the

most amazing people I have ever met and yet, somehow, even more amazingly, I could forget something so special. I finally really understood why Anandapuran had set me the task of remembering these amazing people. The inner dialogue from my ego had blocked them all out of my memory. In Tomas's case perhaps because what he had shared with me was so dangerous to my ego's very existence.

Tomas's influence continued to be a major part of my life since, and I have worked continuously to stop the internal dialogue and see the world. Sometimes I think I have succeeded, sometimes I have, but I have also come to understood over the years that I am trapped in this world we have all imagined together. I know a chair is not a chair, and yet it always is. The sadness that Tomas used to help me stop the world that afternoon has never left nor can it ever, nor would I want it to. Universal sorrow, felt personally, is what offers us hope whilst continuously reminding us of how small and insignificant we are.

Several years later the works of Carlos Castaneda came to my attention and I became an avid fan of his work which was clearly in line with what Tomas had showed me. People doubt the truth of the claims of Castaneda as to his teacher and so forth, but my experience with Tomas at that time shows me with no doubt whatsoever, that even if Castaneda made up his stories, the teachings behind them are most real. More real than we can possibly stand; so real they offer us our best chance of achieving complete freedom. I wish I could shout in your ear just now and stop the world for you, but only you can do that for yourself. My task now is to remember that shout in my own ear and never let its resonating echo ever come to an end.

7. Kabbalah with Dafydd

I first met Dafydd through one of those strange 'book falling off a shelf' moments. I was browsing in a local bookshop and when I pulled a book from a shelf for closer inspection, an adjacent book fell to the floor with a loud clunk. As I bent down to pick up the book, The Mystical Qabalah by Dion Fortune, and to put it back on the shelf, I became aware of someone standing very close to me. I had vaguely been aware of another shopper but I hadn't taken much notice of this person except that he was wearing white trousers (unusual in those days), was tall, and had long blonde hair.

Pointing at the book I was now holding, the stranger asked me: "Are you into this stuff?"

I wasn't quite sure what to answer.

"I don't really know. I think so," I honestly replied. I wasn't sure if he was looking for a positive or negative answer and was purposely vague. Some of the hippies around in those days were a bit edgy, so it was prudent to be cautious about either praising or condemning something, it could provoke an unwanted reaction.

"My name is Dafydd." He reached forward and touched my shoulder. "I'm in a group practising Kabbalah," he said softly but firmly. "You could join us if you are interested."

I was really taken aback and didn't know how to respond. More than anything, my reaction was because Dafydd was actually talking to me. Strange though it may seem, my experience was that in those days there was very little real contact. Hippies were full of peace and love but, when it came down to it, generally very poor at genuine relationship. Here was this tall blonde hippie looking me straight in the eye and engaging me.

I also wasn't sure whether I wanted to say yes or no, but before I could formulate my answer, Dafydd let me off the hook, so to speak.

"Well, man," he said, "it's up to you. The next meeting is at my house Saturday at six, if you want to come, do." He handed me a slip of paper with his address written on it. It was the nearest thing to a business card any hippie had ever given me.

I thanked him and said I'd think about it. I was being dishonest, though, because I never really imagined I would go to his meeting, not in a million years. It was just not my scene, or so I thought. I considered Dafydd's offer the next day and even started reading the Dion Fortune book to see if I would be interested. I did find the book quite good but it didn't stir a deeper intent and, after putting the book down, pretty much forgot all about it.

Saturday afternoon, I'd been shopping in town with Marie and was listening to some new records I'd bought. I remembered Dafydd's offer of attending a Kabbalah group and, looking at the clock, saw that if I left fairly soon I could be there on time. His address was only a few streets away. I asked Marie what she felt about me going and she said she planned to watch a film on TV that night. That helped me make my mind up and, on the spur of the moment, I decided to go. There was no harm in finding out what it was all about, maybe I would enjoy it and, at the very least, it was something different.

Of course, I didn't find out what it was all about at all, far from it. In fact, I thought it was one of the most boring evenings ever. Dafydd seemed truly pleased to see me when I arrived and, although I was nervous, he managed to make me feel quite relaxed. There were five other people there, three men and two women, all of whom seemed pretty unprepossessing. I vaguely knew one of them and hadn't really felt anything for him. One of the women was a friend of a friend, I hadn't met her before but knew some nasty gossip about her. I don't remember the others, except the other woman was very attractive, despite, or perhaps because of, a long scar down one side of her face.

After a brief introduction, Dafydd asked us all to close our eyes and breathe in and out along with his counting. I don't remember what rhythm he used that night, I think it was breathing in to a count of four and out to a count of six. Whatever it was, it actually made me feel more irritated than relaxed or tuned in. We did this breathing for about five minutes, I guess, then Dafydd guided us in a visualisation (or a pathworking as he called it). We went through a gate, over a bridge, into a land of magical palaces. We went to a green palace where we were supposed to talk to a guardian and attempt to gain admission. I never told Dafydd or anyone at the time, but my temple guardian was a green eyed earthworm wearing red and white spotted underpants. He readily let me pass and I spent most of the time imagining myself by a beautiful bubbling brook with a succession of naked women passing by. After the visualisation, when I heard what others had experienced, I decided to keep my experience to myself.

Dafydd said that to do the pathworking, or visualisation, we had been using our astral vision and explained it was necessary for us to develop this special vision so, when we were ready, we could detach from our physical bodies and travel in the astral realms. That was quite interesting to me, but the discussion that ensued was heady and boring, and seemingly interminable. By the end of the evening I was certain that I wasn't interested in Kabbalah and would not be returning to this group. I remember, just after leaving, looking at my watch (it didn't have a strap on it and I kept it in my jacket pocket) and it said 8.30. I had only been there two and a half hours and I'd imagined it was much later.

Being back at home watching TV with Marie seemed much more attractive.

*

When I woke the following morning, I immediately and vividly remembered a dream I had during the night. In the dream I was back in Dafydd's sitting room, where the meeting the previous evening had been held. Unlike the real encounter, however, in my dream the other people were much more interesting. Dafydd, who was actually not much older than me, so in his late twenties at most, was a really wise-looking white haired man of about sixty or seventy. Despite his age, however, he was extremely bright and sprightly. The woman with the scar was also in the dream, she was his partner in the dream. She was naked and her scar ran from her cheek right down to her genital area. The most vivid part of the dream, though, despite such imagery, involved a circle of tarot cards laid on the floor. At one point I was in the middle of the circle holding a magic wand, turning round, pointing slowly at each card. I felt like I was an upturned glass on a ouija board where rather than letters, tarot cards were laid around the periphery. Dafydd and the others were having a séance, using me as the pointer in the ouija. It wasn't frightening, though, it was magnificently bright and, even when remembering the dream upon waking, I felt stronger and brighter from the experience.

I'm not really sure what compelled me to go back round to Dafydd's that morning, but I knew I had to tell him about my dream. I think somehow I felt I owed him that. He was quite nonchalant when I arrived, however, giving the impression he knew I was going to come and wasn't moved by my visit one way or another.

I had not told him about my dream, hardly said more than hello. He led me to his living room and bade me enter the room first. There on the floor was a circle of tarot cards, just as in my dream (only the circle was smaller than in the dream, and Dafydd and I were alone.)

"Stand in the centre of the circle and choose a card," Dafydd said softly.

"But how did you do this? How did you know…"

Dafydd cut me short. "Choose a card, Will – your card."

I felt both ridiculously foolish and surprisingly connected as I stepped into the middle of the cards and, turning round, studied them closely. How would I know which one to choose? I started to worry in case I chose the wrong one but quickly realised there couldn't be a 'wrong' one. Nevertheless, I still wanted to pick the right one! I was sweating all over, and trembling. I vaguely heard Dafydd in the background telling me to breathe and relax, but I was too engrossed in my experience to really hear him let alone take notice of his good advice.

My heart was racing. I felt like I might faint and I knew I just had to pick a card and get out of the circle. Closing my eyes, I turned a little to my left, reached down and picked a card blind. Stumbling forward, I fell to my knees on the floor outside the circle.

Dafydd spoke softly but firmly. "Look at your card, Will," he commanded.

Nervously I opened my eyes and held the tarot card up before me. It was titled 'The Magician' and depicted a man holding a wand in his left hand and something I couldn't make out in his right. On a table before him were other magical symbols.

"The Magician," said Dafydd softly. "You are a Magus, I knew."

I was wondering if it was a card I had chosen in the dream, especially since I had had a wand in the dream and the figure on the card was holding a wand. I excitedly noticed that the Magician, like me, was left handed, I started blurting all this out, excitedly wanting to tell Dafydd about my dream. He stopped me, though, gently placing his finger to my lips.

"Not now, Will, tell me another time." He paused, bent forward, and looking me straight in the face, gave me a somewhat wicked grin. Just for a moment I saw the old man who had appeared in my dream. "Go home and rest now, this work uses up a lot of your energy. Come see me again tomorrow evening."

*

I did rest most of the day, and felt strangely reticent to tell Marie about my experience. When I did share it with her in the evening, over dinner, she didn't seem that interested, which wasn't like her where esoteric matters were concerned, but that evening I may well have been talking about football and other 'boy's stuff' for all the notice she seemed to take. The experience was on my mind all the time, though. Marie went to bed early and as soon as she went, I picked up the Dion Fortune Mystical Qabalah book and tried reading it again. This time it was fascinating and I read over half of it before I couldn't keep my eyes open long enough and joined Marie in bed.

What I had learned from the book was that Kabbalah is based on the Tree of Life, a map designed to help us understand ourselves and our place in the cosmos. The Tree of Life is composed of eleven spheres. The sphere at the bottom of the Tree of Life represents our body, our senses and the physical world around us. At the top of the Tree is a sphere that represents the deepest aspect of our spiritual being, the place where our individuality blurs into union with all other consciousness. The other nine spheres on the Tree of Life, which are situated between these two, have a complex array of paths connecting them. These represent all the other aspects of our being, including, for instance, our thinking and feeling, our fears and judgments, our love and compassion.

At the centre of the Tree of Life is a sphere representing the sun (at the centre of the solar system) and the heart (at the centre of the human system) which is sometimes called Harmony. To experience this sphere is to move beyond words, ideas and feelings, and to find that something still remains, the pure, unattached quality of one's unique individual awareness. A central theme of Kabbalah is that an individual or group using the Tree of Life becomes a living temple of the spirit. Fortune claimed that in the light of Kabbalah the shadows of all transitory things are instantly banished. This was interesting but I didn't feel it told the whole story, nor that it had much – if anything – to do with my experience with the tarot cards at Dafydd's place.

I was agitated the whole next day; I couldn't wait until the evening. Dafydd hadn't specified a time and, although I didn't want to seem too eager, I arrived at his house around 6.30. He was very welcoming, showing me into his sitting room again. This time – thankfully, I thought – there was no circle of tarot cards or any other people there.

I told Dafydd what I had understood of Kabbalah and my sense this was just the surface.

"You are right, Will," Dafydd explained in his usual soft tone. "The relationship between humans and trees stretches back to the earliest history of humankind. Trees have been our protectors, our homes, our foodstuff, they have sustained us, they give us pleasure and occasionally pain. Trees are important to us in our modern world for many reasons, not least because of the oxygen they give and the carbon dioxide they remove from the air we breathe. Trees have always been and still are of prime importance to all life forms.

"Trees figure in our myths, legends and cultures and often represent basic values such as growth, health, fertility, wisdom and strength. On the darker side, their shadowy nature sometimes leads them in myth to entrap and even destroy humans. Trees carry weight in the human psyche, they are powerful and sometimes fearful, particularly when we treat them badly. It is of prime importance in our modern world that we acknowledge and treat trees for what they are, living sentient beings of another order who are on a journey of self exploration just like us."

I had learned the properties of various trees and respected them deeply, particularly through what I had learned from Seamus, and had no doubt about them being fully alive but living in a different time scale from us.

"But what of Kabbalah and the Tree of Life?" I asked.

"Well, in many traditions, a special world tree stands in some central place in the universe and is associated with the origin of all life," Dafydd answered. "The Tree of Life in the Bible is such a tree and is perhaps one of the earliest appearances of the modern Kabbalistic Tree of Life. In the Hebrew myth, the first humans, despite a warning against doing so, eat of the fruit of the tree of knowledge of good and evil which spirals them down into the world of duality. We are right here on earth and yet never fully here because we are trapped in our attachments and identities in a sort of collective dream.

"Kabbalah frames this that through coming to earth, with its attendant difficulties and suffering, we are offered the opportunity for redemption. Unlike some traditions, however, Kabbalists believe this redemption may be achieved through the pleasures of earth as much as through the difficulties. Indeed, Kabbalistic mythology actually stresses that coming to earth is the goal in itself and the most difficult thing to attain. To truly 'be here now' is of course the aim of most Eastern spiritual systems, too."

Now that really was starting to make sense to me and fitted so well with the Eastern traditions I'd been discovering. All the hairs on my body were standing to attention and hanging on Dafydd's every word.

"When we look at a basic tree," he continued, "we see it has many branches and leaves originating from a single trunk, strongly suggesting the development of diversity from unity. This is the origin and template for the evolutionary tree of which we are all part, and for individual family trees. The way a tree comes out from the ground as a single shoot and grows with great diversity and complexity is a potent symbol for the creative growth process both on a personal and collective level. If our life task is to really be here now, to fully 'come to earth', then trees offer us a potent example for this process, being themselves beings that have fully come to earth."

*

As you may imagine, after such a potent start to my Kabbalah studies, I eagerly became part of Dafydd's group and, luckily for me because otherwise I'd have been put off, Dafydd recognised my dislike of the group meetings and, taking me under his wing, taught me individually as well. I still had to attend the group, but as I became more deeply engrossed in the subject, I came to be able to ignore the foibles of the other group members and see us all as on the same path.

At the time, I was still quite politically active and the day I really 'got' Kabbalah was when I brought up the subjects of politics and social justice with Dafydd. I guess I was being challenging, questioning if there was any point in a system like Kabbalah if it remains hidden and esoteric. Dafydd rose to my challenge and supplied what had been for me, in all my questing, the missing link.

"Living on this earth," he said, "we humans have created social and political structures to help us deal with the world itself and with each other. There are, of course, a host of different opinions about how we should govern our societies, what social services should be available to everyone and so on. The rich complex interactions of political difference are both a gift, enabling change and diversity, and a curse in leading to misunderstanding, conflict and war. If we can relate our political world to the Tree of Life, however, it may give us a wider and more spiritual context through which we can understand our place in the scheme of things. It also gives us the opportunity to make clearer and more informed choices when we have the opportunity to take action or in some way to make a difference in our society.

"For a Kabbalist, giving is the highest principle in the universe and central to our practice. When one remains focussed on this central principle, there is no inherent conflict or problem in holding both right- and left-wing viewpoints. The problem arises when such viewpoints hold us, for what has a hold on us also controls us. Conversely, that which we let go of we can direct, making choices appropriate to each situation. Having the width of vision that allows the holding of widely divergent viewpoints is the cornerstone of good Kabbalistic practice. It could be the cornerstone for political and social practice, too."

I remember being truly amazed on hearing Dafydd expound Kabbalistic politics. I felt that simultaneously my old political beliefs which I had held for many years, involving the absolute rightness of a left-wing social position, were being torn down and new, more open and inclusive structures were being erected in their place. It had never occurred to me that I had been holding a fundamentalist position as only people holding right wing views were fundamentalists!

Dafydd hammered home his revelation with an astonishingly apt reference to the Bible. "In The Book of Revelations," he said, "there is a beautiful quote that sums up our political position. It says: 'In the midst of life there is a tree which bears all manner of fruits continuously; and the leaves of the tree are for the healing of the nations.'"

I had to ask him to repeat it several times, I really wanted it to sink in deeply.

"That Kabbalah flourishes," Dafydd continued, "depends upon its relevance in the modern world to political and social issues as well as for individual development and healing. The central principle of Kabbalah, the interconnectedness of all things, involves respect for oneself and equal respect for others. This respect depends upon the acceptance of oneself and others for being as we are. We may intend change but we do not require it. From this ground of mutual respect, a deep relationship can happen, a relationship of equals, rather than relationship built upon hierarchy (someone's better than you and someone's worse), or prejudice (you are the right colour and she is the wrong one). Deep relationships built on a ground of mutual respect are the basis of healing. When we stop trying to be better (hierarchy) or believing we are better or worse (prejudice), and accept ourselves and others for what we all are – equally humble and equally powerful human beings – we free up our ability to interrelate, to understand others for their similarities and differences to us.

"When we connect with the Tree of Life it is as if everything becomes brighter, warmer, stiller, because we are no longer confused, we are free. In this state we relate to others in more appropriate ways. This has to be beneficial for any society or nation and all the interactions between them. This doesn't mean we all have to go round radiating love, harmony and light all the time. Sometimes we will feel awful, some days will be filled with conflict, boredom and distrust. There will be differences between us still, but we will celebrate the differences between us because we are able to understand these differences also as part of ourselves."

"So it is all about become whole, really, about including everything and not rejecting anything?" I asked.

"We need to be whole in ourselves to be able to combine with other whole beings to create a greater inclusion and synthesis. The more of us who move towards wholeness in this way, the more of us there are to work together for the common goal of societal and eventually planetary harmony. We do not even have to work together: knowing and understanding this togetherness exists in itself may release vast potential. Once we are healing ourselves, the best next step in this healing is healing others. The Tree of Life is an ideal agent for this change.

"Listen carefully. We wouldn't be here at all if we didn't have the earth to support the biosphere in which we live. In respecting our planet, we respect ourselves. Further, we add to the flow of positive energies that counteract the negative which brings abuse, famine, war and so on. In respecting our planet, we are co-operating with the unfoldment of life, and passing on to the next generation a place at least as good to live in and perhaps better. There is another sometimes overlooked benefit, too. When we align ourselves and co-operate with earth energies, our good will is returned to us."

*

Dafydd was part of my life for around two years, and he sometimes even called me his apprentice. As well as going to the group (which was always somewhat boring for me) I had regular weekly meetings with him in which he expounded all his Kabbalistic wisdom. He would never tell me where he learned Kabbalah except that he too, like me, had a teacher. He suggested he had been specially chosen by his teacher in the same way he had specially chosen me. I took all this with a pinch of salt. Sometimes I would become quite caught up with this and start to think of myself as special, but whenever this happened something in life would soon bring me back to ground.

One day Dafydd told me that he was leaving town. Apparently his father had offered him a job at a spa resort he had opened in Melbourne. He had never previously mentioned his father or having a connection with Australia. I was really sorry he was leaving but the explanation left me no room to try and persuade him otherwise. In any case, at that time, I had been feeling that perhaps Kabbalah could take me no further. Of course, what I didn't know then was the immense influence it was going to have on my life, nor that I would write books on the subject.

I would have liked to keep in touch with Dafydd but he was very clear when we finally met that it is always best to meet people as new each time, so if we did meet again, not to expect the same personality. We never did meet again and strangely I have always felt this was how it was meant to be. Dafydd had a final gift for me, a teaching of immense relevance.

"Kabbalists believe that creation takes place through a process of fragmentation," he said. "The Source or Creator, an original wholeness, started the breaking of the vessels, in order to know itself, fragmenting itself into the Tree of Life. Our task, as living beings, and microcosms of the original Creator, is then to restore wholeness to the universe. This process of restoring wholeness is to repair the broken vessels. For the individual Kabbalist, the aim of this is to restore a sense of wholeness or perfection to the psyche. Perfection in this sense does not mean everything being perfected, but everything as it is now being seen and understood as perfect in itself.

"You have learned that the middle part of the Tree of Life represents, in one sense, the individual soul. Each individual soul is a holographic replica of the total oneness of the Source. The breaking of the vessels implies the same, that each individual being has a piece of the broken vessels within. Through the process of fragmentation, we each have an individual connection to the original Source. Our task is a process of refining and elevating the individual sparks of soul and re-connecting them to the spiritual level. This reparative process continues whether we co-operate with it or not. As humans, it is our individual and collective task to find ways of doing so,

"Your final task is each and every day to ask yourself what acts are you making or could undertake to co-operate with the process of the restoration of wholeness?"

I never doubted Dafydd would be one of the seven influential people I had been charged to remember, but the exciting thing for me was realizing that the process of remembering these people and their influence was an act of reparation in itself. By recalling them, and giving them their proper place in my memory, I was repairing a split in myself and bringing a deep healing to my psyche.

In recent years we have all become somewhat familiar with the notion that a butterfly flapping its wings on one side of the planet can cause a hurricane on the other side, but I did not have that metaphor to use back then. If I had, though, I would have embraced it because it describes exactly how I felt at that time, like a butterfly flapping my wings, not intended any distant effect and yet aware of the potential of my activities. My journey, rather than just being for me, was for everyone else too: when we 'flap our wings' we have a responsibility for doing so with awareness and consideration for the effects our actions might induce. On the positive side of this, if we behave ethically and send out good vibes, then to know this might have positive knock-on effects beyond our own sphere is astounding. It was as if all the previous teachings took on a new meaning, no longer a selfish pursuit of individual enlightenment but part of a human, worldwide quest for self-knowledge, in which each individual plays his or her specific, unique and irreplaceable part.

8. Mysticism with Dorothy

I had not been intentionally trying to put the seven important people in any particular chronological order. Somewhere along the way in the process of remembering them, however, I started doing so. I was twenty-four years of age on that fateful afternoon when Anandapuran came to my flat and twenty-five when we met for the second time and he brought me the task of remembering the seven most amazing people I had met in my life. Justin, the first, I met when I was seventeen and he set me on a Buddhist quest which literally saved me from sinking further into severe depression; I was just nineteen when I encountered Seamus and was initiated into a Celtic Magic Circle and taught the importance of being at one with the earth; twenty when Gabriel introduced me to Subud and shared latihan, teaching me to surrender to life however it unfolds; twenty when Ashe opened up the Lord to me, introducing me to Sufism; twenty-one when Tomas brought me to inner silence and helped me see the world as a Shaman; and twenty-two, when I met Dafydd and he kindled my interest in practical Kabbalah, reconnecting me to my deepest spiritual and political awareness. By the time I had remembered these six encounters and reflected back over the meetings and what they might mean for me, I had grown rather weary of the task. At the time it seemed rather pointless and my faith, if it was that, in the significance of Anandapuran in my life was waning. I gave up the task and, although occasionally I considered it, I was truly stumped to imagine who the seventh was, assuming I couldn't count Anandapuran himself.

The truth is, I was rather pre-occupied with something else, too. Although Marie and I had enjoyed our first couple of years in the Yorkshire countryside, after that we increasingly became dissatisfied there and wanted more stimuli in our lives. This state of affairs brought great pressure to bear on our relationship, and we started arguing a lot. We both felt like we wanted to escape and projected the role of jailer onto the other.

Marie was very bright intellectually and in just one year, whilst working full time, she took two A-level examinations (English and Mathematics) attending once-a-week evening classes, and achieved an A grade in both. She was offered a place at Sussex University and she and I moved in the summer of 1977, when I was twenty-seven, to a flat in Brighton. There was rather a poignant catch to the move, though. Marie and I had decided to separate when we re-located from Yorkshire, but when it came closer to the move, and separation, Marie felt increasingly anxious about being in a new place on her own. In the end, I agreed to move with her to Sussex for her first year at University, to help and support her over the transition. This was no hardship, Marie and I were still good close friends and it wasn't as if I was planning anything particular. My intention was to go and live in Bristol, where I had some good friends, but if I delayed it for several months, it really made little difference.

At the time I was doing some freelance writing and running a book import business, specialising in rare books on the esoteric. Making an income from writing is never easy, and the book business was too small to bring in more than a basic income. I could move both businesses, as it were, to Brighton, but I needed to generate more money. Marie had her grant, but it was pretty small, so between us we had just enough (again!) but no excess. I wasn't thinking of Anandapuran's prediction and his teachings about the circulation of money, I was caught up in a much more mercenary frame of mind, and wanted to earn plenty of money so I would have sufficient for my move to Bristol.

I quickly found a job that ideally suited me, at least for a short while. I became a baker's delivery man; my job entailed getting to the bakery by six in the morning, loading up my van, then driving to make deliveries, mostly to shops. I had other tasks to do after I returned to the bakery, sometimes going out with extra goods, sometimes helping in the actual production, but always I finished at one p.m. This was ideal for me; I didn't mind getting up early at all, I had been doing so for several years for my morning meditations anyway. Then finishing at one o'clock would give me the rest of the day free, or so I thought. Of course, I hadn't counted on the stress of the physical labour involved and how much energy I would use. I didn't generally feel too good in the afternoons, and mostly just hung out doing very little at all. The worst part of the time, really though, was the journey to work in the morning. The bakery was a twenty-minute motorcycle drive from where we lived. Being winter, the mornings were dark, very cold, even icy, and about two miles of my journey took me along the major route to town, a very busy and narrow road with lorries zooming down it. I only had a small motorcycle and spent that time in a state of near terror – every morning for a few months.
Despite this, I enjoyed much of the time living in Brighton. Marie and I found an acceptable rhythm, but it became clearer and clearer that we really did have to separate. Also, I really didn't want to be – couldn't energetically afford to be – a baker's delivery man for much longer, either, it was starting to really sap my energy.

One weekend, about four or five months after we had moved, I was away visiting some friends, and when I came back I found Marie in a particularly agitated state.

"You won't believe this," she said excitedly, "we have had

a letter from the estate agent and the owners would like us to move out and terminate the lease early."

My first response was to take this negatively, a hassle I could do without.

"No, listen, Will," said Marie. "They are offering us money to move out early!"

It turned out to be a gift from spirit, to say the least. I went into the bakery the next morning and gave them a week's notice. Marie had already sussed where she could move, having been offered a room in a large student house. I called my friends in Bristol and they were fine for me to come and stay with them until I found my own flat. Best of all, Marie and I now each had enough money to support us fairly reasonably. I certainly had enough to pay a deposit for a flat and see me through a couple of months in Bristol.

*

My last Friday at work for the bakery, I was sent out midmorning to deliver a deluxe birthday cake to a farmhouse somewhere on the edge of town. It took me a little while to find it but finally I pulled up at the door and rang the bell. A grand old farmhouse, it had beautifully landscaped grounds that were just a little on the wild side which added to their attractiveness. Seeing such places was a part of the bakery job I enjoyed, not least because I also met some interesting people. To be honest, I was most interested in the young women I met, but on this day rather than a young woman, I was to meet an old gentleman who was to help me remember my seventh amazing person.

The door opened and a white haired, slightly bent old man told me to bring the cake through to the kitchen. I didn't take much notice of him and, having carefully lifted the cake from the back of my van, I followed him through a wood panelled hall into a warm, bright kitchen. After I'd gently put the cake on a large kitchen table, he asked me if I would like a cup of tea and some biscuits so I accepted.

Pointing to me to sit at one end of the kitchen table, the old man sat deliberately opposite me, staring at me in a somewhat disconcerting fashion.

After asking my name, the old man introduced himself as the General. "And you can call me the General," he said firmly. "And what are you looking for?"

"What do you mean?" I asked.

"And I can tell you are not only a baker," he said, somewhat short-temperedly.

I noticed he always seemed to start each sentence with an 'and'. "So?" I responded.

"And so, what are you looking for?"

"Well, peace, happiness, enlightenment, sex, a new life."

"And so you are just like everyone else, then."

"I suppose so."

The General wouldn't let it go at that, though. "And so, what are you looking for underneath all that?" he asked.

I thought for a moment. The most obvious answer would be love, I supposed, or some other abstract quality or another, I wasn't sure. My task from Anandapuran came into my mind, however, and, thinking nothing of it except to give the old man an unexpected answer, I replied: "The seventh person I need to remember."

The General's response to this was even more surprising. "And then look to your very beginning." Just that, clearly, looking straight at me: "Look to your very beginning."

My mind was swirling. His words had some effect on me that I didn't understand and, on my more rational days, I assumed he didn't intend. I asked him to explain what he meant, but he acted like a doddery old man then, and changed the subject, more than once. I quickly finished my tea and biscuits and left. I drove back to the bakery in a daze, said goodbye to my colleagues, then went back to Marie's and my flat.

"What is it, Will?" asked Marie as soon as she saw me. "You look exhausted, really pale. Are you okay?"

"Listen, Marie," I said. "Do you remember Anandapuran?"

"Of course. Often."

"I think I met the someone general today!" I explained.

"What? What do you mean?"

"You remember Anandapuran saying I'd meet someone general, well I met someone today who called himself the General."

"But what does this mean?" Marie asked.

"I think I have understood who my seventh amazing person is."

Marie looked as excited as I felt, and I think also went pale. She knew what a struggle I had had trying to remember another amazing person and how disillusioned I had become.

"An old man told me it today: look to your very beginning, he said."

"What does that mean?"

"My very beginning, who was there?"

Her face lit up. "Your mother!"

"Exactly!"

My mind was in a spin, well more, my whole body. Not only had I never once thought of my mother as an amazing person (except as being my mother) but the idea of her being the seventh – and really by far, the most important person for me to remember would have seemed ludicrous to me if I had considered it before. But I hadn't, and now I felt completely disorientated, and yet, at the same time, felt released from something. I had no doubt that my mother, Dorothy, was the right person for me to remember. Of course, I wouldn't have been alive without her, but that was a given, and I just couldn't remember what it was about her, or my relationship with her, that I needed to recall. Or, more accurately, couldn't quite remember, it was as if something vitally important dwelt at the edge of my consciousness. I kept trying to recall all my exchanges with her and, the more I recalled, the more agitated I became. I think I was a real pain with Marie but she was very patient with me. Perhaps it was because we only had a few days left together, but I like to think it was because she had met my mother so knew something of what I was going through. My agitation brought me face to face with my life and what I planned ahead. I kept asking myself the question who am I and more importantly, what am I for? Am I for sitting here looking at this beautiful view, seeing seagulls flying over wet fields behind our flat in Brighton? Am I for moving to Bristol and starting a new, I-don't-know-what life?

One afternoon, Marie was out at college and I fell into a strange trance. Through the raindrops on the window I could see there was a golden yellow and bright pink cloud above and near the horizon. I felt totally naked, confronted with my fragility in the face of the unknown.

I fixed the image in the window. I looked out of it. The world stopped. I vividly recalled the words of Tomas. "That's all there is really," he had said, "raindrops on a window." His words again had a profound effect on me and I became aware of there being innumerable worlds that underlie our apparent reality.

As before with Tomas, only even more deeply this time, for a moment – an undefinable moment in time – everything became crystal clear.

A little later Marie came home and found me still sitting in front of the window. "Is something the matter?" she asked, looking at me with concern.

"Not really," I replied. "Well, its not that anything's the matter, I'm just remembering something." I wasn't crying but tears were pouring down my face.

Most people think their mother is special, don't they? Of course, but what was amazing about my mother was not at all to do with her being my mother, it had everything to do with her unusual and magical energy. That she lived her life to the full, non-stop, always energetically engaged, might be enough in itself. Right through my childhood I remember her filling her days up – completely – and yet still being able to find time for herself. Most nights she only slept about four hours and she found that enough. As well as all the housework, she did a full time job, socialized extensively with neighbors and friends, supported members of her extended family, dealt with her somewhat difficult husband, and brought up her son with masses of love and attention.

It has taken me many years to recall the most important aspects of my interaction with her which I had to do before being able to confidently step into my life and fully come to ground. These meetings with idiosyncratic representatives of various spiritual paths led me to this discovery, aided me in remembering just what my mother had told me about life and spirituality. In fact, remembering was made much more difficult because I have had to put aside all my memories and feelings about her as a mother. During her life, I had just shrugged off all she told me because I didn't understand it's importance.

*

"Thy will be done. Climb down. Climb down from the middle of unrest," she said to me whilst I was in a trance-like state.

My mind just wandered.

We were playing my favourite childhood game. 'Froggie.' I must have been five years old. My mother was doing her special frog voice. "Hello Will. This is Freddy Frog here," she started. "What do you want for your tea. I'm having pond weed for mine. What are you having for your tea?"

"I don't know," I replied. "Mummy hasn't made it yet."

"That's all right, she will. Maybe you can help her. What would you like for your tea?" Freddie asked in his croakiest voice.

"I don't know." I was thinking hard but I could quite get anything to come into my mind.

"Your mummy wants to tell you something." She coughed. Her voice came to normal. "I've got something very important to tell you. I'm going to tell it to you now and I'm never going to tell it to you again. So it's very important you remember it. So you do remember I'm going to just touch you by here." She bent across the table and just lightly touched me with her hand round the back of my neck. An overall feeling of calm came over me.

Of course, I trusted her completely, I had no reason not to. I liked her hand round my neck, where she touched me. Then she said, "That's it. And you must always remember that. Now when I take my hand away you'll forget everything except that I've told you it."

"What?" I was confused. Then she took her hand away and I wasn't confused. I just knew something.

"So," croaked Freddy Frog. "You'll have chips for tea. Hooray here we go."

"Hooray," I said. "Hooray!"

So what was it she told me? I could see my mother so clearly in my mind's eye, it was as if she was actually present. I could hear her voice telling me something I had to remember. I felt five years old again. It felt for a moment like someone was watching me, witnessing me more like, someone enormous, so big they encompassed the whole universe and yet were completely contained in my own heart.

This is what I have remembered, finally after years of recovery and reparation. I could only fully enter the world Dorothy had showed me when my everyday view of life stopped and I was seeing everything as it truly is, a place of more amazing wonders in every person and every event than we usually imagine in our wildest dreams. Our purpose in being alive is to engage fully with life in all its splendor. This is the essential understanding of all religions and spiritual approaches. It is exemplified clearly in the Kabbalistic teaching that our task is to fully come to ground, and the various spiritual paths that recommend connecting to inner silence as more significant than anything else. Tomas and Seamus with their belief in earth magic and shamanism had supplied the key to this, but I could only use this key when I remembered the simple teaching from my mother – that life is to be fully engaged with. As simple and profound as that.

I was completely ready now to move on to Bristol and whatever my life brought next. I felt fortified by all the teachings I had been led to receive and I stepped into my new life with renewed confidence and purpose. Having remembered the seven amazing people, I could now fulfil another part of Anandapuran's original prophecy for my life.

I moved all my belongings to Bristol, left them at my

friend's house, and then drove the hired van back to Sussex. I spent one last night with Marie, now in her shared lodgings. We both felt sad but absolutely right about the end of our couple relationship. The following morning, with some tears, I bade a final farewell to her and went into Brighton to catch the train to London, then on to Bristol. You know, I would not have been at all surprised on entering a carriage on that train to find Anandapuran sitting there. Perhaps I hoped for that, but the message was clear without his physical presence. I imagined that he vigorously shook my hand and we laughed together, a laugh of happiness and sadness and something more – of vision, hope and purpose. My new life really was just beginning.

*

My life after moving to Bristol took many new and unusual turns and in the years between 1978 when I moved there, and 1985 when I moved to London, as Anandapuran predicted, I met several more especially amazing people, mostly, this time, women. During that period, I trained as a psychotherapist, wrote my first book on Kabbalah and found myself deeply involved in life in a way I had never felt before. Best of all, though, I had a new girlfriend who I loved deeply and felt was, hopefully, to be my life-partner.

Shortly after meeting her, I planned to take her to meet my mother but sadly my mother died before this could happen. In fact, the very weekend we had planned for this we actually went to her funeral.

Just a couple of weekends before, I had my last meeting with Dorothy. She was sitting on her bed in the lotus posture, bald and even skinnier than her usual skinniness, suffering the pain of her advanced cancer and the side-effects of treatment. I had visited her only a couple of weekends before, but the deterioration in her health was now rapid.

We smiled at one another.

"You've met your star," she said brightly.

"You mean my girlfriend?" I asked.

She nodded assent.

"You'll meet her in two weekends time," I added happily.

Mum said nothing but looked at me very deeply.

"Look," she said, nodding towards the window." It was pouring with rain outside. "That's all there is really," she said, "raindrops on a window."

As was her knack, her words immediately shocked me into an altered state of attention. I remembered Tomas having said exactly the same words to me many years before and my experience in Brighton. Using the same words – was it a co-incidence? – my mother created the same effect in me that Tomas had back then, a profound sadness that brought me into contact with the other world that underlies this one. The profound sense of incompleteness that goes for me with this state washed over me.

"It is time," said Dorothy, "I'll show you my death." I sat in front of her as she curled her bony hands round the back of my neck and pressed on the base of my skull.

*

A few days later, back home in London, I received the news that mum had died. That evening, whilst preparing for bed, my girlfriend became very agitated. At first she wouldn't say what was disturbing her but finally I managed to persuade her to tell me.

"I seem to be receiving a message from your mother," she said, hesitatingly. She seemed a very grounded person and I knew that she wouldn't be making up such an idea. She was really embarrassed, though, and concerned she was having a silly fantasy that would upset me, or insensitively intrude upon my grief. She had never even met my mother, so why would my mother send a message for me through her, she thought.

I asked her to tell me anyway, it didn't matter whether it was 'real' or not.

Leaning forward, she took my head in her hands, just as my mother used to whenever we had had an argument or after she had been telling me off for something.

"But you are still my son," she said, the exact words that my mother used at those times.

Dorothy always told me that if there was any way she could communicate to me after she died, she would send me an unambiguous message.

Now of course it is possible to find all sorts of explanations for this but realistically, for me anyway, all of those explanations are more fantastic than an acceptance of the message being from my mother.

I received another message from Dorothy exactly five years after her death (to the day.) I had been aware of the anniversary and spent some time that day reflecting upon my mother. That night I had a dream which I recorded in my journal the following morning:

'There is a loud whooshing sound, almost deafening, and it feels like I am in a thick treacle, but I am awake in the dream. I can see a figure sitting with its back to me on a bed, cross-legged, thin and wiry, wearing a skull cap. This person is also in the thick treacle and only with great difficulty is managing to turn to look over her left shoulder towards me. It is my mother, only a male version of her, old and wise looking. Slowly she raises her left hand and points. My gaze follows to where she is pointing and I can see a pretty little blonde girl of about three sitting in a colourful push-chair.

'My mother speaks, in a slow, deep resonating voice.

'"Things are different, now," she says.'

*

Books by Will Parfitt from PS Avalon

The Great Circle of Time

Using will and imagination we have the power to heal not just on the physical but on deeper genetic levels. These are the final entries in the journal of a traveller in alternative realities who partners a mysterious pilgrim and, through dream-like experiences on magickal pathways, heals wounds from ancient traumas.

This Beautiful Earth

This book contains many stories that have a spiritual take on gardening that can connect you to a deeper, older archetypal rhythm, the rhythm of nature and the earth herself, something collective that we grasp when we put our hands deep into the soil – or should that be soul?

The Something and Nothing of Death

Death is ever present throughout life and the more we learn to face this fact the more death becomes a wise advisor who encourages us to live life more fully. To make a relationship with death is to make a commitment to self-evolution and overcome unnecessary fear.

Psychosynthesis: The Elements and Beyond

Psychosynthesis is a practical system that integrates principles and techniques from many approaches to personal and spiritual growth. This book presents a deep and practical exploration of the subject and reveals Psychosynthesis as the psychology of choice for now, not just for the individual but also for the larger world in which we live.

Kabbalah For Life

This book explores this fascinating and ancient tradition and how relevant it is to our everyday lives. With practice, Kabbalah deepens our connection to life and to our underlying spiritual journey

For details of these and other books
by Will Parfitt visit

www.willparfitt.com

available from Amazon
amd to order from all good bookshops

Kindle editions also available

www.ingramcontent.com/pod-product-compliance
Lightning Source LLC
Chambersburg PA
CBHW020111020526
44112CB00033B/1176